Tom Paine, Revolutionary

Tom Paine, Revolutionary

by Olivia Coolidge

CHARLES SCRIBNER'S SONS
NEW YORK

Contents

Introduction

It is tempting to compare Tom Paine to another famous figure who devoted his life to social revolution brought about by political means. Karl Marx, unlike Paine, was a great constructive thinker whose ideas have influenced our whole century. At the same time, he lacked Paine's direct and forceful eloquence. Thus Marx had little popular appeal and small success in his lifetime. The closest likeness between the two men is their inability to control or direct an actual revolution. In other words, both were men of ideas rather than action, the difference being that Marx was the thinker and Paine the propagandist.

Unquestionably Marx was the greater man, since the real credit for the liberal ideas of Paine's time is not Paine's at all. Yet we should not be led to undervalue him, merely because we are suspicious of propaganda. Unlike too many of his kind, Paine was not marketing wares for personal profit. He truly believed that his principles were important to mankind, and history on the whole agrees with his judgment. In other words, we have to give Paine credit not merely for eloquence, but for a sense of what was vital. We may admit that his vision was limited, but he did have a power of selection particularly striking because he lived in a confused, revolutionary era.

These, then, are the talents of Paine, that he was clear-sighted and possessed an extraordinary gift of persuasion. As a person, he is a fascinating example of the human species, since he was at the same time both great and petty, admirable and repulsive, strong and weak. This contrast in him seems to have diverted the goodness, which was genuinely part of his nature, into unusual channels. He made few intimate friends, but learned to love in people the qualities that are common to us all. He cared less for individuals than for human beings.

Thus it was that Paine expressed his true self not by what he did, which was often ill-judged, but by his ideas. His failings, all too human though they were, did not betray his principles or interfere with his devotion to humanity. They merely rendered him a little ridiculous, a little unpleasant, and ineffective in most of the practical situations he confronted.

Fate seemed to exaggerate his difficulties by casting him up on American shores in 1774, only a few months before the outbreak of the Revolution. It then returned him to Europe in 1787, less than two years before the French Revolution. Thus in neither case did he have a clear understanding of the pressures which had built up the explosion. He was free to contemplate the principles involved, understanding these all the more clearly because he was not tied down by local prejudice. He was mistaken, however, in supposing that either revolution really embodied the ideals which he saw in men's hearts. The golden age of the common man, which he prophesied for America, is something still not achieved in our day. The French Revolution broke the power of the old regime, but established in its place a tyranny of a new sort and militarism more formidable than the world had yet seen. In neither case did Paine foresee what was going to happen, and his inexperience is surely a chief reason why he did not.

Everybody who worked with Paine perceived that he was lacking in industry, tact, good sense, and political discretion. His manner was a little too unpolished and his personal habits too sloppy. As an employee he was almost always unsatisfactory. There even hung about him a faint suspicion that he was not honest, mainly because he was muddled in his behavior. Finally he had lofty ideas of what was due to himself and was capable of pressing his merits endlessly on other people.

All these drawbacks mattered little, since actually Paine was right about himself. He really was a man of principle, a lover of humanity, a true believer in the rights of human beings, a defender of the helpless and the poor. He really did tackle human problems in a spirit of hope, convinced that they were soluble and inspired to present them in a way which would be understood and remembered. Other people might possess the human touch; Paine was better without it. He was set apart to speak to all mankind.

1737-74
The Years in England

Joseph Pain, maker of ladies' corsets, appears in history on January 29, 1737, at the age of twenty-nine, when his wife presented him with a son whom they named Thomas. A corsetmaker plied a respectable but humble trade, and Joseph Pain was not an impressive figure. He lived in Thetford, a country town of about two thousand people, not far from Harwich on the east coast of England, where he occupied a small brick house forming part of a continuous line along the main street with doors opening directly onto the roadway. It had two rooms upstairs and two below, one of which was shop and workroom. In the eighteenth century, corsets were an important part of ladies' wear; but they were solidly stitched and worn until they fell to pieces. Thetford was not a wealthy neighborhood, so that such articles would often be handed down from one generation to another. Pain made enough to support his family, which was luckily small. He also owned a farm of an acre or two, which helped him to manage. He lived in the same house all his life and died in his seventies without having saved enough to keep his wife from want.

Pain had a gentle nature, as befitted his profession; and he was a Quaker. It followed that he was sober and industrious, but that he differed from his social superiors in matters of religion and had no roots in the parish.

These drawbacks may have been in part compensated for by his wife.

Frances Cocke Pain, who was eleven years older than her husband, had married at thirty-seven and must have settled back long before to be an old maid. We are told that she was sour and eccentric, but her unequal marriage and long, frustrated spinsterhood may have accounted for that. Unmarried women had no profession save that of unpaid servant in the house of a brother or brother-in-law who felt under no obligation to be considerate. Frances Cocke, who was the daughter of an attorney and respectably Church of England, must have been desperate indeed to have married a Quaker corsetmaker of such poor prospects. Evidently she brought no dowry with her of any importance, save her social pretensions. Of these obscure and ill-matched parents was born the revolutionary whose name was to become a household word in three great nations.

The discord between Frances Pain and her husband soon showed itself in the upbringing of their son. Mrs. Pain was not quite strong enough to defy Quaker meeting and the marital authority of Joseph by taking Tom openly to church. She had, however, a sister who was willing to instruct the boy in church doctrine, and to get him confirmed. The result was that from his early years young Tom was exposed to two theologies, each strongly critical of the other. The result was less to confuse him than to develop a natural talent for simplification and for making up his own mind on important issues.

He was about eight years old when his aunt read to him a sermon on the doctrine of the atonement, explaining how God sent His only son into the world to die for the sins of all mankind. When the reading was over, Tom went outside and, with such intensity that he always associated the moment with the step into that yard, he rejected the whole conception. If an earthly father, unable to get revenge for wrongs that were done to him, were to kill his innocent son, then surely, young Tom reasoned, he would deserve to be hanged. It was an insult to God to think of Him acting in this fashion.

Many people have found the doctrine of the atonement a stumbling block, but seldom at eight years old and in opposition to their elders. It is true that Joseph Pain and the Quaker community had possibly criticized his mother's church in the hearing of young Tom, who preferred the Quakers and was fond of his father. But however his decision was reached, there was a moral courage in it which was characteristic of Paine in later life. For the present he called himself a Quaker, and yet he was not entirely convinced by the Quakers either. Long afterwards, he reflected on how dull the world would be if God Himself had been a Quaker and had given us Creation without bright flowers or singing birds. And before he was out of his teens, he had broken any formal connection with the sect.

Thetford was a small place; but it once had been important and still possessed a good grammar school which had been founded in the sixteenth century by a local magnate. Frances Pain and her husband might disagree on religion, but they were united on the advantages of education. Poor as they were, it cost them a good deal of sacrifice to keep their son in school; but they did so until he was thirteen. To be sure, they would not let him study Latin because of the pagan philosophies of Virgil, Ovid, and other Roman writers. Tom was perfectly satisfied with this because it saved him drudgery, while he managed to pick up the gist of the authors studied, no doubt by consulting the handwritten translations which freely circulated in all such grammar schools to lighten labor. Meanwhile, he turned his attention to history, mathematics, and science, which suited his practical mind.

He was a bright boy and not without imagination. Indeed, he tells us that he had a talent for poetry, which was discouraged by his Quaker upbringing. Unfortunately for this claim, a few examples of his verse have survived, none very much more poetic than the epitaph he wrote at eight years old for a pet crow:

"Here lies the body of John Crow
Who once was high, but now is low.
Ye brother Crows, take warning all,
For as you rise, so must you fall."

These lines, which merely parrot pet phrases of the day, are doggerel, not poetry. They do, however, scan and probably were a source of great pride to the young author and his parents. A naïve vanity which was part of the boy's make-up was encouraged until he began to fancy he was a poet. Alarmed at this tendency, his father discouraged his efforts; and presently Tom turned his attention to mathematics and science, which better suited his mind. But his impressions that he knew Latin literature and had poetic talent were too precious to be dispensed with. Without a qualm in later life he laid claim to both.

Much sympathy has been wasted on Paine because when he was thirteen he was apprenticed to his father. In eighteenth-century England he was lucky to have the chance of learning a trade. Apprenticeship normally cost about forty pounds, a sum which Joseph could not possibly have scraped together. The best he could do for his son was to train him as a corsetmaker, which would enable him, if he did not care for Thetford, to find work in a larger world. Young Tom, who was a thin, sharp-featured boy with a high color and a pair of great dark eyes, now beginning to look eagerly at life, undoubtedly accepted this fate as a matter of course because he had always expected it.

Four years later when he was seventeen, he was less resigned. Anybody more unsuited for the ladies' garment trade could scarcely be imagined. Naturally impatient, little interested in women, eager for adventure, and not at all industrious, he dreamed of making his fortune in more romantic ways. One of the masters at the grammar school had been to sea and liked to tell his classes the tale of his adventures. Harwich, a flourishing seaport, was only some thirty miles off, a mere day's journey. In 1754 there was war with France; and Harwich was filled with privateers all hopeful of making their fortunes by preying on French commerce. Casting aside his Quaker principles, young Tom ran off to do the same and enlisted aboard the *Terrible,* whose captain, appropriately enough, was surnamed Death.

Perhaps he left a note explaining his intentions. At all events, his father followed, horrified that Tom should consider joining with bloodthirsty men to slay fellow creatures. So mildly, yet persistently did he argue that he prevailed over the boy. They returned home together; and Tom may be thought to have had a lucky escape, seeing that the *Terrible* was defeated shortly after, losing a hundred and seventy-five out of her crew of two hundred.

Two years later he ran away again and made a voyage

in the *King of Prussia* under a Captain Mendez. He did not
make his fortune, and we know nothing whatever about
his adventures. Some have even suggested that he never
really joined the *King of Prussia,* but invented the tale to
show he got the better of his father. This may be so, but
Paine never spoke much about his past, since he was
always more interested in the ideas of the present.

To some extent these ideas may be traced back to Thetford. As a relic of past grandeur the "freemen" of the
borough had privilege of sending members to Parliament.
These freemen in medieval times had formed a closed
corporation, extremely jealous of admitting new members to their privileges. As Thetford dwindled and families
died out or moved away, the freemen were reduced to
thirty-two. Their votes were up for sale; and the Duke of
Grafton, landlord and magnate of those parts, had them
"in his pocket." He put up the candidates, and the town
elected them as a matter of course. Pocket boroughs like
Thetford were a national scandal; and it mattered little
that Grafton, a reformist Whig and an intelligent man, selected sensible people. Their votes were known to be cast
for his interests in Parliament, not for Thetford's. Meanwhile large industrial towns of recent growth had no repre-
sentation, and demand for reform was becoming wide-
spread.

Joseph Pain, as it happened, had been made a freeman
of Thetford about the time his son was born. Thus he had
a vote, but he had also an inside view of the timidity and
corruption of the electors. Besides this, the boy had other
chances of seeing how the common people were governed.
Thetford was one of the places where assizes were held with
all the usual pomp of visiting judges, official wigs, scarlet

gowns, and formal processions. Justice was not necessarily corrupt, but it was unfeeling. Savage punishments were inflicted for trivial offenses, and the poor were always at a disadvantage. Next to the tiny Quaker meeting-house stood the jail, and outside it were the pillory and stocks. Whipping and even public hanging were not uncommon.

Clearly Paine's sympathies even from boyhood were with the underdog, and against the established Church of England, the well-fed justices, and the parade of mayor and aldermen. City government was pretentious for the size of the shrunken town; and no doubt it was in the hands of a few, of whom Joseph Pain can hardly have been one. Tom Paine did not believe that he would ever have the smallest voice in what went on.

As young Tom grew up, he soon became weary of Thetford, which indeed could barely support his father and mother. In 1757, he left for London, where he worked for a Mr. Morris as journeyman corsetmaker. He stayed for over a year, though probably with indifferent success; for Paine never had a taste for drudgery. He bought a pair of globes for the study of astronomy and physics. He attended philosophical lectures. He developed an interest in natural science which brought him in contact with one or two distinguished people, notably Dr. Bevis, an astronomer and member of the Royal Society, and George Scott, who was a member of the Board of Excise.

Paine did not stay in London long, perhaps because he had relatives in Kent. Soon we find him settled in Dover at the shop of a corsetmaker called Grace, an even better name than Pain for a maker of corsets. One year later, in 1759, he set up a shop of his own on borrowed money in Sandwich, Kent. In September of that year he married

Mary Lambert, maid to a Mrs. Solly, who was a woolen draper's wife. Mary was an orphan, and clearly the marriage did not improve Tom's circumstances. In 1760, he moved to Margate, where he hoped to do better. Mary died there in childbirth, and he soon planned to move again.

Four changes in four years do not suggest that Paine cared for his trade or its modest prospects. Twice he had failed to establish a shop of his own, and one wonders whether his relations in Kent were tired of him. It seems quite probable that he had settled there because they had helped him, possibly by lending money. At all events, he had begun to look about him for a chance to set himself up in another profession. Mary Lambert's father had been an excise officer, so that she probably encouraged him to try this profession. Presumably through his acquaintance with Scott, he was accepted by the excise, which brought him back to London for a short course of training.

Excise officers of the period were government officials collecting taxes on a number of goods, of which beer, wine, and spirits were the chief. Such taxes were an easy way of raising revenue; and the government, involved in a series of expensive wars, depended on them. The steeper they became, however, the more profit there was in smuggling and black-marketeering. The revenue officers, ill-paid and too few in number to control the traffic, were either bribable or easy to outwit. The consequence was that a revenue official was an unpopular man throughout his district. His exactions—and he must of course raise some taxes—fell on the poor who had no influence or power to corrupt him. Even if he were honest, he sold the poor widow's cow or her sticks of furniture because she was friendless. The jovial innkeeper, in league with half the countryside, was harder to catch and far more dangerous to meddle with. If Paine had deliberately sought a profession calculated to arouse his pity for the poor or outrage his sense of justice, it is hard to see how he could have chosen much better.

In 1761, Paine was appointed an assistant officer, and somewhat later he was employed to measure brewers' casks to estimate their tax. Eventually in 1764, he found himself a full-fledged officer on the lookout for smugglers in Alford. His district was large, and he had to keep a horse, so that his salary of fifty pounds a year was reduced by expenses to about thirty-two, which works out at twelve shillings and sixpence a week. This was a poor living wage even for a bachelor, but it contrasts favorably with the eight shillings and sixpence Paine had received as a journeyman corsetmaker. At least he could tell himself he was rising in the world.

Unluckily, he was hardly more successful in his second profession than he had been in the first. In 1765 he was discharged from the excise for stamping dealers' papers without inspecting their stock. According to his own account, this was no more than a routine way of coping with rounds so long that they could not be properly covered. But Paine at no time of his life was a steady worker, and it is likely that the fault was partly on his side. At all events he was dismissed and had to find employment as a corsetmaker again for eight shillings and sixpence a week.

He did not stay long with his old trade, since a few months later we find him teaching English grammar and composition at the academy of a certain Mr. Noble in London. He had risen to nine shillings and sixpence a week, but the profession of an assistant schoolmaster was only slightly removed from drudgery. Pretty soon, he moved to another school, but in the meantime, he had written an apology to the Excise.

"Honourable Sirs: In humble obedience to your honours' letter of discharge bearing date of August 29, 1765, I delivered up my commission and since that time have given you no trouble. I confess the justice of your honours' displeasure and humbly beg to add my thanks for the candour and lenity with which you at that unfortunate time indulged me. And though the nature of the report and my own confession cut off all expectations of enjoying your honours' favor then, I humbly hope it has not finally excluded me therefrom, upon which hope I humbly presume to entreat your honours to restore me. The time I enjoyed my former commission was short—an officer only a single year. No complaint of the least dishonesty or intemperance ever appeared against me; and if I am so happy as to succeed in this humble petition, I will endeavor that my future conduct shall as much engage your honours' approbation as my former has merited your displeasure. I am your honours' most dutiful humble servant." He signed this letter "Thomas Pain," not having yet adopted the final "e" which appears occasionally in earlier records, such as the register of his parents' marriage.

Whatever we may think of the tone of this petition, which repeats the word "humble" half a dozen times, it at least did the job for which it was intended. Paine was reinstated in the excise service and, after refusing a job in Cornwall, a notoriously dangerous spot for collectors of taxes, was appointed in 1768 to Lewes, near Brighton, in Sussex. Here, for the ninth time, he started again.

Paine was thirty-one when he arrived in Lewes, and so

far he had done little with his life. He was slender, five feet eight inches tall, high-colored and dark-haired. His nose was large and prominent, his mouth wide but well-shaped. His most striking features were his brilliant eyes, a dark blue-black. He was quick in movement, always in a hurry, incisive and witty in speech, and of outspoken radical opinions. He made his rounds once more on horseback, carrying a measuring stick covered with figures and wearing an ink bottle slung from his buttonhole. In general, he gave the impression of having abilities which had so far found no outlet. He was not a persistent worker, however; and though not a drunkard, he liked his glass of brandy in the evening.

He found lodging at the Sign of the Bull, a medieval tavern which, after many transformations, had been converted into a tobacconist's shop by Samuel Ollive. The Bull was a magnificently timbered house with two satyrs carved on the outside posts. Downstairs were a kitchen, sitting room, and shop, while above them were two stories of bedrooms. Paine had the best of these, comfortably large and looking onto the street. Apparently he found the Ollives congenial, and he settled down to make his home in Lewes.

He soon joined a circle of friends who used to gather in an informal club at the White Hart Tavern to spend their evenings in talk. Lewes was a small town, but it had its radicals and its ambitious young men with literary pretensions. A good deal of verse was written, including some more productions from Paine. Thomas Rickman, who has left us a picture of those days, went later to London and made some reputation as a poet. Paine produced a number of essays or poems on subjects which happened to interest him at the moment. These doubtless were read and discussed; and though they did not contain much of importance to us, they helped to establish their author as a man with literary ambitions. But his dominating quality to his friends was his love of argument.

They called Paine "Commodore" because of his experience at sea on the *King of Prussia*. They had splendid debates with him and often got so heated that they invented a joke to calm themselves down, handing round an old Greek Homer, which they called the "Headstrong Book," and which was presented to the most obstinate debater, usually Paine.

There was a great deal to talk about. The poverty and injustice which Paine beheld in his work affected him strongly, the more so as he was little removed from poverty himself. In later life he prided himself on having never, despite the temptations of his office, oppressed the poor. From birth he had been outside the established order, and he regarded its faults with increasing resentment. Corruption in politics, for instance, was characteristic of this age and especially galling to those who were left without a vote. The close alliance between privilege and the Church of England was widely challenged by the nonconformist tradesman class, of which Paine was a member.

Hovering on the brink of the industrial revolution, England was humming with activity. Old problems called for new solutions, while fresh complications were met as often as not with a sense of outrage. Those in power resented change, while those without it thought solutions easier than they were and blamed the selfishness of the aristocracy.

It was a violent age, when savage punishments were inflicted for trivial crimes, but the vast majority of criminals went uncaught. Private philanthropy had done much to raise the standard of literacy through village schools. Better farming methods were slowly improving the laborer's diet, and medical discoveries were having some result on public health. But the weavers of Spitalfields, the boatmen on the Thames, the tailors, glass-grinders, or coal-heavers of London were caught by rising prices and poor pay. Strikes were common and riots easy, since the government had no organized forces at its disposal in London.

Social unrest was not new in Paine's day, but it was being spread through the country by the development of news sheets which were intended to catch the attention of a wide reading public. A century earlier, these sheets would have been pamphlets on the Protestant religion or the claims of the House of Stuart. Their style and their learning would have fitted them for an educated group. The present papers, often violent in their opinions, were aimed at men like Paine or prosperous tradesmen who resented being kept out of government circles.

Conspicuous among the sheets which circulated in the coffeehouses of London and provincial taverns like the White Hart was *The North Briton,* written by John Wilkes, a radical member of Parliament and a furiously intemperate man. Wilkes was in opposition to the court cabal of George III, to buying and selling Parliamentary votes, to pocket boroughs such as Thetford, and in general to interference with what he called men's liberties. Paine, who was a reader of *The North Briton* and deeply moved by its arguments, had followed with resentment the arrest of

Wilkes for going too far in treasonable language, which necessitated his flight to the Continent and brought about the suppression of his paper.

In 1768, the very year Paine came to Lewes, Wilkes returned to England under an amnesty. He was promptly elected to Parliament by the County of Middlesex, which was equivalent to greater London and possessed a reasonably popular franchise. Parliament was outraged. Not only was Wilkes a radical of the most violent sort, but his personal character was not respectable. He was deeply in debt, had been indicted for treason, and had won his seat by rabble-rousing tactics. By a majority vote, Parliament declared his election null and void.

This act put Parliament in the wrong and raised Wilkes to the position of a martyr to political persecution. The County of Middlesex was almost the only place in the country where members of Parliament were truly elected by popular vote. Its outraged citizens immediately returned Wilkes in a fresh election. Parliament, persisting in folly though it had no legal power to refuse the Middlesex member, forced a third election and a fourth with the same result. Mob violence broke out several times, and Wilkes became a popular national champion.

The natural result was to bring other radicals of widely differing views into alliance with Wilkes. Most reliable among these was Horne Tooke, born John Horne, of a good middle-class family. His father had been a well-to-do poultry dealer, while his brother became a famous market gardener who is said to have developed the strawberry for commercial growth. As a youth, Horne had wanted to be a lawyer; but his father's resources and sympathies did not permit this. Instead, Horne found himself an Anglican parson, unfitted by temperament for religious duties, and pouring his ardor increasingly into political channels. He was a worthier character than Wilkes, whose real interest was self-advancement.

In 1769 Wilkes and Horne (who had not yet adopted his second surname as a compliment to a close friend) founded the Society for the Defence of the Bill of Rights, with a mixed program which included extension of the franchise and reform of the jury system, together with justice for Wilkes and an inquiry into government handling of the recent riots on his behalf. To this they added a vague declaration of sympathy with the American colonies, plus a denunciation of the East India Company, reflecting the dislike of the London poor for the great London merchants.

Having thus attempted to please everybody, but most especially Wilkes, they gave real significance to their movement by setting up a central committee to correspond with provincial groups which supported their program. This marked the first appearance in England of a political society which was founded on a broad popular base and had as its object revolution or reform. For the moment it did not score any success except in the matters closest to the heart of Wilkes, who was elected both member of Parliament and Lord Mayor of London in 1774. He took his seat at last—and achieved nothing. His organization soon collapsed, disillusioned by his use of its funds for his personal ends.

The days when Wilkes was the most important man in England coincided, as we have seen, with Paine's residence in Lewes. He was too independent a man to join societies founded by other people, or even to organize his own. The

White Hart club did not become the headquarters of a
branch of the Society for the Defence of the Bill of Rights,
but the arguments with which the tavern resounded were
often political. All his life Paine was a man to whom conversation was more important than serious study. He
needed the cut and thrust of ideas in order to work out his
own, especially as he liked to put these in simple terms,
suspicious of the jargon by which more learned men impressed their fellows. Here at last in the White Hart we
can see the real Paine develop, not the rolling stone or the
unreliable employee, but the good crony, the lover of talk,
and above all the passionate devotee of political science,
the man who believes that constitutional change must
benefit the poor.

In the meantime, Paine had at last begun to put out
roots in Lewes. His landlord, Samuel Ollive, died in 1769;
but Paine stayed on in the big bedroom, while the widow
and her daughter Elizabeth ran the shop. In 1771, he
married Elizabeth Ollive, enlarging the shop to include
groceries and other odds and ends, quite possibly wares
which he hoped to pick up cheap through his connections
with local tradesmen. Unfortunately, his business judgment was as usual bad. The shop never did very well and
was soon in difficulties.

Paine naturally still had his profession, and the collapse
of the shop meant little to him because he had found a
cause. The officers of the excise were transferred a good
deal, so that they formed a network of friends and acquaintances all over the country. Paine's trenchant criticisms of his job spread widely among them, for it was not
only his friends at the White Hart who were impressed by
his conversation. Besides being outspoken, he had con-

structive ideas. At his urging, a petition for more pay was drawn up and circulated for signature by excise officers throughout the kingdom. A contribution of three shillings per man was levied for expenses, and the five hundred pounds raised by this means were turned over to Paine. Thus supported on a far more lavish scale than he had ever thought possible, he plunged into the work of lobbying.

It is fair to say of Paine that though not indifferent to money, as indeed the poor seldom are, he was never extravagant in his personal wants. In this respect the excise officers could hardly have entrusted their fund to a better man. Moreover, he was tasting the joys of leadership for the first time, so that enthusiasm bore him along. His first achievement was to produce a masterly pamphlet setting forth the plight of the excise officers. His argument was that corruption is a necessary result of underpayment. It results in recruitment of inferior men, while at the same time it forces superior ones, who may have strayed into the ranks, to lower their standards because of the needs of their own families. In describing the privations which the excise officers suffered on fifty pounds a year, he proved himself a convincing master of detail. Finally, in his general summary, he rose to eloquence which is clear and unpretentious, yet effective. "He who never was ahungered may argue finely on the subject of his appetite . . . But poverty, like grief, has an incurable deafness which never hears." The greatest pamphleteer of the century had found his voice.

Paine's next step was to request a leave of absence in order to present his cause in London. For a period which stretched into several months he remained there, first get-

ting his paper printed and perhaps outfitting himself in a
decent suit. He then obtained introductions of every sort
and haunted the houses of members of Parliament or the
Board of Excise, not to mention those of other influential
people. He even included Benjamin Franklin, who as
agent for New York and Pennsylvania and one hardly
knew what else, had fingers in every possible pie.

These were exciting times for an obscure officer of the
excise, and it seems scarcely surprising that Paine used
them to the full. He even, for instance, sent a copy of his
pamphlet to the poet Oliver Goldsmith and obtained a
meeting with him in which he made an excellent impression. One never knew from what direction publicity might
come, so that policy and personal advantage went hand
in hand. Paine returned to London without the permission
of his supervisors, enjoying himself and also avoiding his
creditors in Lewes.

He ran a fine campaign for a good cause, but it had a
single drawback which might have occurred to Paine before he started. Everyone disliked the excise officers,
whether they made themselves a nuisance or not. They
were despised for their corruption, and they were hated
for their oppression of the poor or for the inconvenience
they caused to "decent" smugglers. Paine might be as
eloquent as he liked about their miseries, but no one cared
a jot. Plenty of people who were far more widely pitied
were worse off. It was thus impossible to put any organized
pressure on Parliament. Nor was Paine in any case the
man to find supporters, since influence, not eloquence,
was needed for this purpose. Finally, his moment was ill-
chosen. Still struggling with the debt of the past war and
vainly attempting to raise revenue from the reluctant

colonies, Parliament was in no mood to grant a bonus which came directly out of the national pocket. The petition was doomed from the start.

As soon as the petition was rejected, Paine's own fortunes collapsed. The shop in Lewes was already bankrupt, and a public auction had disposed of Paine's household furniture, his stock of tobacco and groceries, his mills for grinding snuff and tobacco, and a couple of crates of cream-colored stoneware which he had presumably picked up as a bargain. Meanwhile, he had made himself known to the Board of Excise as a troublemaker, so that they were glad to discharge him. It is characteristic of Paine that when he had a cause to push, he took little account of what he spent. No doubt the five hundred pounds had been used up on behalf of the excisemen, while his own resources may have been pledged as well. At all events, his supervisor reported to the Board that he dared no longer show himself in Lewes on account of his creditors.

The situation was particularly hard on Elizabeth Paine, who was left in Lewes to face bankruptcy, while her husband tried to push his cause in London. Apparently she did not share his enthusiasms; the marriage had been a business partnership rather than a match of affection. It did not survive the collapse of his fortunes. Elizabeth retired with her mother to the house of a brother who was a watchmaker and reasonably prosperous. As far as we know, she never saw her husband again, though Thomas Rickman says that he occasionally sent her money. At all events, apropos of a legal arrangement which came up in 1800, Elizabeth stated that she had heard nothing of Paine since 1774. We need not believe this literally, since his name was by then a household word, while Elizabeth was well known to be his wife. It is said, however, that she never would allow her husband to be discussed in her presence.

For his part, Paine was almost equally silent about his wife and their reasons for separation. A bachelor by preference, he never seemed to miss her. It even suited him in later life to say that he was married as a pretext for avoiding other women. He was far more interested in the political arguments of male company than in flirtation. In 1774, he nonchalantly shook off the dust of Lewes, shrugged away his previous professions, and at thirty-seven and for the tenth time started again.

1774-76
Common Sense

By 1774, Benjamin Franklin had been representing the American cause in England for ten years and had come to the conclusion that he was achieving nothing. His sympathies were naturally with Paine, whose own attempt at lobbying for a reasonable reform had ended in failure. Different though they were in many respects, Paine and Franklin had in common a middle-class background and a keen intelligence which resented condescension from those born to power. It is true that Franklin had risen to wealth and the company of his betters by his own industry and good judgment, whereas Paine had not so far shown similar qualities. Franklin, however, had seen Paine in action at a time when his powers were beginning to make themselves felt. He had evidently liked him, and their acquaintance had been strengthened by a common interest in experimental science.

In the age of the scientific amateur, great discoveries were possible for an intelligent man who took nothing for granted, was prepared to persevere, and was ingenious in devising experiments or constructing apparatus. Franklin was such a man, and Paine would have liked to be one. He was fertile in ideas and had grasped the principle that progress depended on experiment. As we have seen, on his first appearance in London he had made his way into scientific circles. So far, however, his unsettled life and meager resources had given him little chance to develop his talents. Thus to Benjamin Franklin, Paine at thirty-seven was still a young man of great promise whose slow start might be due to conditions in England rather than his own fault. Franklin urged him to begin once more in the American colonies, where he would surely be offered the chance for which he had been waiting so long.

Paine was perfectly ready to agree, since the thought of going to America had occurred to him even before he met Benjamin Franklin. Separated from his wife and independent of his parents, he now felt that he had nothing to keep him in England. Accordingly, in September, 1774, he set sail for Philadelphia on the *London Packet,* bearing a letter from Franklin to his son-in-law Richard Bache which read as follows:

"The bearer, Mr. Thomas Paine, is very well recommended to me as an ingenious, worthy young man. He goes to Pennsylvania with the view of settling there. I request you to give him your best advice and countenance, as he is quite a stranger there. If you can put him in the way of obtaining employment as a clerk or assistant tutor in a school, or assistant surveyor, of all of which I think him very capable, so that he may procure a subsistence at least, till he can make acquaintance and obtain a knowledge of the country, you will do well and much oblige your affectionate father,

Benjamin Franklin"

Surprisingly enough, Paine, whom we last saw completely destitute, had found enough money to book himself a berth on the *London Packet.* It was well for him that he did so, for the ship's hold carried a hundred and twenty indentured servants, among whom a typhoid epidemic broke out. Five died, and the disease spread through the ship, attacking Paine, who might well have died also, had he lived in the hold with the others. As it was, when the *London Packet* docked, he was too ill to get out of bed. It was known, however, that he bore a letter from Benjamin Franklin, whose very name worked magic. A certain Dr. Kearsley drove down to the dock and carried Paine to his own quarters, where he did not leave his room for the next six weeks.

Philadelphia in 1774 was a town of thirty-five thousand, larger and wealthier than any other place in the thirteen colonies. It was well laid out with many shade trees and gardens and had a few streets paved for carriages or with narrow brick sidewalks. In general, its appearance was spacious and gay compared to the older English towns. Wooden shopfronts were brightly painted, and their swinging signs were gaudy. There was nothing somber about the city except on Sundays and holidays, when its Quaker inhabitants put on their browns and grays, reserving silver buckles, gold lace, and heavy silks for common occasions. This was an arrangement with which Paine, half a Quaker himself, might feel at home.

No one who had come from England to America in 1774 could possibly have done so without having heard of the resentment of the colonies against their mother country. It would have been difficult for a man far less intelligent than Paine to have avoided making up his mind one way or the other. Nor could he have been unaware of the many incidents which had brought the colonies close to a state of war. What he lacked in the situation was first-hand knowledge, but Philadelphia was the best place for acquiring a general picture. Toward the end of 1774, the first Continental Congress dissolved, but the second gathered there in May, 1775. Most of the American leaders were to be found taking their ease in the London Coffeehouse or the Indian Queen Hotel. Paine, who had taken lodgings in a private house on Market Street, frequented these places to pick up acquaintances or listen to talk. Thus almost from the first he formed connections among men who were to be leaders of the new nation.

Meanwhile, Richard Bache and other friends of Franklin had been busy on his behalf. Introductions led to tutoring jobs and thence to more congenial employment. In January, 1775, Robert Aitkin, who owned a bookstore and printing shop, was launching a monthly called the *Pennsylvania Magazine*. Paine wrote an introductory essay in praise of the New World and modern times, and he was shortly afterward appointed editor for fifty pounds a year. Under his guidance the magazine began to prosper, increasing its circulation from six hundred to fifteen hundred in three months.

Most of the contents of the *Pennsylvania Magazine* were written by Paine, signing himself for the sake of variety "Atlanticus," "Aesop," or "Vox Populi." Practical science caught his eye, and he wrote a description of "a new electrical machine." In a later number he explained a "new method of building frame houses." Always on the alert to praise America, he paid a visit to the fossil collection of the Library Company of Philadelphia and wrote an article called "Useful and entertaining hints on the internal riches of the Colonies." These contributions were spiced by essays and poems which he had written in

Lewes, such as for instance an elegy on the death of General Wolfe or an allegorical tale about Alexander the Great. He added reflections on unhappy marriages, which may have struck a personal note, and a denunciation of dueling. Only occasionally did he come out in praise of the rebellion which broke into open warfare after Concord and Lexington.

On the whole, the *Pennsylvania Magazine* was not exciting. This, in part at least, was Aitkin's fault, for he was afraid of his editor's radical opinions. The most serious article which Paine wrote at this time was published in the *Pennsylvania Journal*. It was an outspoken denunciation of African slavery, which Paine forthrightly said was against nature and the dictates of the heart. He even added that Americans could hardly complain of English efforts to enslave them while they tolerated slavery among themselves.

Other people had written against slavery before, but Paine's was the first voice to denounce in blunt language what many knew in their hearts to be an evil. Possessing few friends so far, he was not concerned lest he offend them. Apparently it never occurred to him that he might make enemies. In fact, it was typical of Paine that when he held an opinion, he did not care in the least what others thought. This was a trait which was to bring trouble upon him in later life, but for the present it won him a friend. Benjamin Rush, the noted Philadelphia doctor, so admired the article that he sought out its author with congratulations.

Paine's slavery article was published in March, 1775. By May, the outbreak of fighting in Massachusetts and the assembly of the second Continental Congress presented Paine with a cause which drove the plight of the Negro out of his head. In England, he had belonged to the radical section of the public which supported the American colonies as part of its opposition to the state of affairs at home. Tyrannical bumbling was just what Paine expected of the English government. Without a qualm, he was instantly on the side of his new countrymen and even prepared to take an extreme view. If he had no ties binding him to America, he also had no connections which attached him to England.

Unfortunately for Paine, the cautious Aitkin had not the temperament of a national leader. It was all very well to write about new machines or the resources of the colonies in the *Pennsylvania Magazine*. Such subjects were patriotic and progressive without being controversial. The war, on the other hand, was a matter about which many were still undecided, especially the wealthy merchants, often pacifist Quakers, who depended on their trading connections with England. Paine managed to insert an ode to *Liberty Trees;* and he also remarked that, though as a Quaker he was pleased to negotiate with England, he was glad he had a musket in case no agreement could be reached.

This sort of downright statement was not welcome to Aitkin, and the two were increasingly not getting on. Paine was one of those writers, not uncommon, who hate to sit down to work. A long period of mental struggle seemed to go on inside him before his ideas became clear enough to express, so that it was not easy for him to produce a whole magazine once a month. At first he padded it with the articles which he had brought over from England. Soon, however, these ran out, while he lost interest in anything which did not bear on the struggle between England

and the American colonies. The result was that the magazine was late in getting to the printer, so that Aitkin had to
pursue his editor with reproaches. He began to perceive
that Paine was naturally lazy, and he noticed other things
as well. On one occasion he forced Paine to come home
with him and sit down at once to his work because the
printers were already waiting for their copy.

"He accordingly went home with Aitkin," writes another
printer to whom Aitkin told the story many years later,
"and was soon seated at the table with the necessary apparatus, which always included a glass and a decanter of
brandy. Aitkin observed 'he would never write without
that.' The first glass put him in a train of thinking; Aitkin
feared the second would disqualify him or render him un-
tractable; but it only illuminated his intellectual system;
and when he had swallowed the third glass he wrote with
great rapidity, intelligence, and precision; and his ideas
appeared to flow faster than he could commit them to
paper. What he penned from the inspiration of the brandy,
was perfectly fit for the press without any alteration or cor-
rection."

This anecdote seems authentic, though in fairness to
Paine we cannot measure the size of the brandy glass or
estimate how far Aitkin might exaggerate what he clearly
thought to be shocking. At all events, it shows us a side
of Paine which may give a better explanation for his lack
of success in life than is provided by his poor origin or the
class system of England.

By July of 1775, Paine and Aitkin had reached the part-
ing of the ways. Paine was constantly asking for cash, and
he evidently considered the magazine a waste of the time
which he was anxious to devote to a better cause. He was

glad to resign; and a few months later we find him busy
with experiments "for the purpose of fixing some easy,
cheap, and expeditious method of making Salt-Petre in
private families." He had drawn up a scheme for a "Salt-
Petre Association" to supply the public magazines with
gunpowder.

Nothing came of this activity, and perhaps his money
ran out. Meanwhile, however, Benjamin Franklin, who
was back in Philadelphia, conceived the notion that Paine
was just the man to write a history of the conflict from the
American point of view. Because of the importance of
setting the colonies right with the rest of the world, Franklin was eager to have a first volume come out without delay. He had misjudged Paine, whose industry was by no
means equal to this gigantic task. Instead of refusing it,
however, Paine planned to surprise Franklin with a composition of a sort which suited him better.

The Continental Congress, waging war by every means
in its power, had authorized the construction of a navy and
was forming a committee to negotiate alliances abroad. In
other words, its acts were those of an independent government, though it was careful to do them all in the name of
the king. Independence was seen as a necessity by Franklin, Samuel Adams, Washington, and a few others; but
need for unity kept them silent about it. Most wealthy
men and natural leaders in their communities were connected to England by many ties. It was, for instance, about
this time that the Philadelphia Quakers published a manifesto strongly affirming their loyalty to the king.

Moderation and caution would not do for Paine, who
had brought over strong radical ideas from England. Before he even sailed for America, a series of articles had

been published in London entitled: "American Independence the Interest and Glory of Great Britain." If Paine
had not read these, he would probably have seen them
when they were reprinted in America in 1775. From the
beginning, he had been a convinced supporter of American
independence, which he discussed in detail with Benjamin
Rush.

Dr. Rush, who was by nature a crusader, entirely agreed
with Paine, though he was cautious about expressing his
opinion. He was, he pointed out, tied to Philadelphia,
where he had to consider his practice before taking up so
unpopular a cause. Paine, on the other hand, could live
where he pleased and had nothing to fear from the hatred
to which a publication might expose him.

In agreement with this casual view of his prospects,
Paine at once set to work on a pamphlet arguing the cause
of independence. Every time that he brought a fresh chapter to Rush, the doctor was delighted by its eloquence. He
later remembered especially a sentence which Paine struck
out on revision. "Nothing can be conceived of as more ab-
surd than three millions of people flocking to the American
shore, every time a vessel arrives from England, to know
what portion of liberty they shall still enjoy." It is indeed
a fine example of Paine's highly readable style whose
lively pictures appealed to men with every degree of education.

Paine struck the right note from the beginning by en-
titling his pamphlet *Common Sense*. It was privately
printed, and he surprised Franklin with the first copy in
January, 1776. His instinct in writing it had been a sound
one, and it soon proved that he had done his cause more
service than if he had embarked upon a formal history.

Paine opens with an argument which sums up in vivid language the current liberal views on government. There was nothing new about these, though Paine denied that he got them from philosophers such as Locke, from whom they originated. He worked them out, he said, for himself— which surely means that he formed them through discussion with people who had in fact read Locke. Paine's method of acquiring his opinions meant that he had met them not in the logical order of a reasoned treatise, but in the vivid cut and thrust of argument on current subjects. It is easy to see that he was a born propagandist, a man with an extraordinary talent for popularizing ideas. But his picturesque style, clear thinking, and ready understanding of other people's motives were greatly developed by this method of self-education. Locke's ideas were not so much distorted as given a freshness which made them seem peculiarly Paine's own.

Government to Paine is a necessary evil forced on society by human wickedness. Its purpose is to give its subjects security, and the government which does this in the simplest way is the best. But the British constitution is so complex that the nation can suffer for years without discovering what has gone wrong. Its very worst feature is the monarchy; for natural ability does not descend with hereditary rights, and kings may be fools. The claims of the present royal house may in any case be dismissed by a quick view of history, starting with the original ancestor, William the Conqueror. "A French bastard landing with an armed banditti and establishing himself king of England against the consent of the natives, is in plain terms a very paltry rascally original." Tracing the fortunes of

William's successors, Paine reaches the conclusion that monarchy has "laid the world in blood and ashes."

With such a government, Americans should not seek to be reconciled. Paine argues that the colonies always have suffered and will continue to do so by the connection. Nor has Britain any real rights over America, seeing that "Not one third of the inhabitants, even of this province, are of English descent."

"I have never met with a man, either in England or America," Paine exclaims, "who hath not confessed his opinion that a separation between the countries would take place one time or other." He points out that fifty years later it might well prove impossible to form a single nation when the colonies have developed each in its own way. "Now is the seed-time of continental union, faith and power." Now all are united by a great cause. "The sun never shone on a cause of greater worth. 'Tis not the affair of a city, a county, a province, or a kingdom; but of a continent—of at least one eighth part of the habitable globe."

Finally, the course of the war makes necessary a formal declaration of independence. How can France or Spain give help to a mere rebellion? Why should they wish to do so if America's only purpose is to reunite with England, thus strengthening their powerful adversary? "Until an independence is declared, the continent will feel itself like a man who continues putting off some unpleasant business from day to day, yet knows it must be done, hates to set about it, wishes it over, and is continually haunted with the thoughts of its necessity." Surely Paine's personal character gives an edge to these words, which carry conviction.

Paine's first plan had been to publish *Common Sense* as a series of letters to the press, but he soon discovered that his subject was too hot for editors to handle. Even the *Pennsylvania Journal,* which had printed his slavery article, was not receptive now. Dr. Rush had earlier warned him that there were two words which he must avoid if he valued his safety, namely, "independence" and "republicanism." His argument depended largely on both. It was clear that if he wanted to write on these subjects, he would have to find a printer for himself.

The arrangement that he finally made with a printer named Robert Bell was that Paine would pay any losses and would share the profits equally with Bell. But, disdaining to make any money out of what he considered was a public service, Paine assigned his share of the profits to two officers of the continental army, who were to spend them on warm mittens for the troops going to Quebec.

Common Sense came out in January, 1776, in a two-shilling edition which was exhausted in two weeks. In fact, the pamphlet was an immediate sensation, surprising everyone, including its author. Many people who had never thought of independence before were instantly converted by the vivid arguments of Paine. It seemed indeed as if he was only saying what everyone had been waiting for. War is a great changer of opinions, so that mere liberty had perhaps already proved too vague a thing to fight for. Paine's fine conception of the "seed-time of continental union" offered Americans a positive goal which they at once perceived was in their grasp.

Paine had done the colonies an extraordinary service by presenting them with a cause worth fighting for. But perhaps he was equally useful in providing an enemy worth fighting against. A great part of Paine's genius was his perfect understanding of how common men must feel on political issues. With this he combined a remarkable ability to popularize an idea by expressing it vividly. In *Common Sense* he instinctively perceived that war requires hate, and hate is easiest to feel in personal terms. Accordingly, throughout the treatise the actual villain is not the British constitution, but the monarchy; not Parliament, but George III. On that dull, conscientious figure Paine focused all the resentment aroused by injustice, folly, brutality, and war. So captivating was his eloquence that the new conception was immediately popular, and it severed emotional connection with England at its source in the British Crown. Thus Paine focused hatred and gave determination to continue in a struggle which must lead to independence.

The success of *Common Sense* led immediately to a quarrel with Bell. Paine, always a little grasping about money because in his experience it was hard to come by, claimed thirty pounds for his mittens. Bell replied that expenses in his small edition of a thousand had swallowed profits up, so that he was lucky to break even. This dispute was embittered by the fact that the two had entirely different objects. Bell, with a best-seller on his hands, wanted to print a larger edition at a profit. Paine, thinking in terms of his cause, was merely anxious to lower the price and get his pamphlet distributed widely.

In the end, Paine enlarged *Common Sense* by an appendix and an address of protest to the loyal Quakers of Philadelphia. With these additions, he gave it to two other printers, guaranteeing their expenses for six thousand copies, which were to be sold to a bookseller at eightpence

halfpenny each and to be retailed at a shilling. Bell, meanwhile, went ahead with an unauthorized second edition of
the original; and battle was shortly joined in advertise-
ments for the rival versions. The upshot was that Paine
found himself out of pocket by about thirty-nine pounds
for the second edition, a sum which looks formidable
enough compared to his usual income.

After the reduction in price, the pamphlet sold faster
than ever and was received with wild enthusiasm. To be
sure, not everyone was swept away. John Adams, for instance, coolly remarks that Paine "came from England
and got into such company as would converse with him,
and ran about picking up what information he could concerning our affairs, and finding the great question was
concerning independence, he gleaned from those he saw
the commonplace arguments, such as the necessity of independence at some time or other; the peculiar fitness at
this time; the justice of it; the provocation to it; our ability to maintain it; etc. etc." Thus spoke the scholarly mind,
but even Adams was compelled to admit that he could have
written nothing in "so manly and striking a style." He adds,
however, not without reason, that Paine was better at
pulling down than building up. Paine's concrete proposals
for forming a new constitution were at once too liberal
and too vague for Adams' cautious mind.

That reluctant praise was extorted from John Adams
in spite of his evident dislike of Paine will testify to the
power of *Common Sense*. In particular, the army seized
upon it with eagerness. The British press reported that
officers were reading it to the ranks. Washington admitted
its wide influence, while an officer in the American camp
declared that its arrival was worth five thousand men to

the patriot cause. Its effect on the Continental Congress
was equally startling. Almost overnight leaders began to
announce in public the desire for independence which
prudence had hitherto led them to conceal. The way was
thus opened for the Declaration of Independence, which
duly followed.

Common Sense had not been signed, but Paine made no
secret of his authorship. Both under his own name and
also as "Common Sense," he found himself the embodi-
ment of the Revolution. More surprisingly yet, his popularity in France was enormous, both in liberal circles out
of hatred for the royalist regime, and at court out of hatred
for England. *Common Sense* in actual fact soon sold more
copies in France than in America, and it takes its place
among the publications which prepared the way for the
French Revolution. The pamphlet even spread to Latin
America, where the later independence movements of
Venezuela, Mexico, and Ecuador owed much to its eloquence. In one short piece of masterly prose Paine had expressed the longings of his age in terms understandable to
the plainest men of his time, yet with an eloquence which
is highly readable today.

1776-78
The American Crisis

While Paine was working on *Common Sense,* the war had shifted from New England to New York. Since he had no one in the world dependent on him, Paine thought it his duty to take part in the fighting. Accordingly, he enlisted in August, 1776, in the Pennsylvania division of the Flying Camp, a body of ten thousand raised for the purpose of being sent anywhere they might be needed. He was stationed in New Jersey, and was shortly offered a post on the staff of General Nathanael Greene with the rank of brigade major. In this capacity he moved to Fort Lee, New Jersey, across the Hudson River from Manhattan. He soon had his baptism of fire, as Lord Percy moved troops into the Harlem Plain and threatened Greene's outposts there.

On November 20, the enemy cut off the fort by landing in boats seven miles to their rear. Fort Lee was not strong enough to hold out. Indeed, its ammunition and light artillery had already been removed to strengthen New Jersey; and its abandonment was only a matter of time. Greene retired with as much baggage as his wagons would carry across the Hackensack River, where he joined Washington. Paine marched with Washington's army in its retreat across New Jersey, which culminated in the crossing of the Delaware on December 8.

Paine was not by temperament a soldier. "Not all the

treasures of the world, as I believe, could have induced me," he writes, "to support an offensive war, for I think it murder." Nor did he pretend his first experience of being fired on did not make him nervous. He performed his duties adequately but spent much of his free time arguing with a kindred spirit about mathematics. He had little chance to see action during the retreat.

From the beginning, Paine had acted as a war correspondent for the *Pennsylvania Journal,* sending it vivid little accounts of incidents which might serve to bolster morale. Soon, however, he perceived that he had more to say than could be thus expressed.

In the first place, he had come to feel admiration for General Washington, whom he rightly saw as the only possible military leader. "There is a natural firmness in some minds," he notes, "which cannot be unlocked by trifles, but which, when unlocked, discovers a cabinet of fortitude." Such a man was Washington, never appearing to full advantage except in difficulties and in action. Paine was aware that doubts of Washington were beginning to be felt in Philadelphia as the retreat went on and Howe came nearer. He deliberately set himself to put the General in his true light, so successfully that much of Washington's early reputation may be traced to Paine.

In the second place, he understood the conflict from the military point of view. In temperament, to be sure, he presented a great contrast to the cautious, pessimistic Washington. While the General was writing that the game was up unless a new army could be speedily recruited, Paine was saying, "We have the prospect of a glorious issue." Both, however, meant the same thing. Both had seen Washington's army disintegrate at Newark, for no better reason than that the time of many enlistments was up. Both realized that all depended on the recruitment of long-term soldiers instead of militia. Washington, however, merely pressed this problem on the Congress; Paine, the propagandist, tackled it himself.

He started a new pamphlet while the army lay at Newark. This was eventually to become the first of thirteen which, collected together, are known as *The American Crisis*. He signed it "Common Sense" and had it printed in Philadelphia on the 19th of December, just before Washington's Christmas victory at Trenton.

"These are the times that try men's souls," began the first *Crisis* paper in ringing tones. "The summer soldier and the sunshine patriot will, in this crisis, shrink from the service of their country; but he that stands it *now* deserves the love of man and woman." America can and will win if men stand firm. The army has found its true leader and needs but reorganization, which is now taking place. Howe's advance across New Jersey is no real victory for him; it has but increased his difficulties. "I thank God, that I fear not. I see no real cause for fear . . . By perseverance and fortitude we have the prospect of a glorious issue; by cowardice and submission, the sad choice of a variety of evils."

Such words, and from the author of *Common Sense,* set hearts aflame. The *Crisis,* it was said, was read to every corporal's guard in camp, while its opening sentence was in the mouth of every recruit to the army. Reinforced by Washington's dramatic coup at Trenton, it banished the depression into which many had sunk. Not unnaturally it cemented a friendship between Paine and Washington. One Sunday early in January they attended Quaker meeting together at Princeton. It must have been warm for the time of year, since Paine left his overcoat in charge of his servant. When meeting was over, however, he discovered that the man had run off with the precious garment. Washington jokingly reminded him that one had to watch as well as pray, but he also pressed on Paine his own second coat to make up the loss.

Paine was already at work on a second *Crisis* in the form of an open letter to Richard, brother of General Howe, who had been sent to America in 1776 with an offer of pardon to all who laid down their arms. This gave Paine a fine opportunity for personal abuse of George III, and also for describing in dramatic detail the ravages of General Howe's army in New Jersey. "Why, God bless me!" he cries in outraged scorn, "what have you to do with our independence? We ask no leave of yours to set it up; we ask no money of yours to support it; we can do better without your fleets and armies than with them."

The publication of the first *Crisis* paper really put an end to Paine's service with the army. He had become too valuable to waste his time in a profession unsuited to his genius. He saw this himself and was glad to take up an appointment as secretary to the commissioners who were to negotiate an Indian treaty at Easton, Pennsylvania. This was a temporary office, but others were soon to follow. In April, 1777, he was elected to a Committee of Correspondence of the Whig Society of Philadelphia, a band of patriots whose chief object was to arouse feeling against the American Tories. His third *Crisis* paper was accordingly directed against these, with particular reference to the loyal Quakers of Philadelphia. Though impractical in daily affairs, Paine was always fertile in suggestions for carrying out his plans. He now proposed a tax of ten to twenty per cent be levied on all property, with exemptions granted to any who would take a loyalty oath. Thus those who leaned to the British side to protect their investments would speedily find that it profited them to change.

Two days before the publication of this *Crisis,* Paine was nominated secretary to the Committee for Foreign Affairs by John Adams. It was an appointment which did not please everyone, since already Paine was a controversial figure. Pennsylvania was debating a new constitution at this time, and its proposals were far too democratic to please the moderates. Paine in fact had nothing to do with the constitution, since he had been away with the army while the convention had been sitting. He spent his time, however, with Timothy Matlack, Franklin, Benjamin Rush, and other local patriots with radical views. Outspoken as he always was, he had become conspicuous among them and an object of hatred to the opposite party. Congress, in part affected by this local situation and in part by the tendencies of the times, was splitting into factions. Paine was charged by his enemies with being a turncoat who had originally written against the American cause. He was called a drunkard, too; but neither accusation could be proved. The appointment was eventually confirmed.

This post not only commanded a salary, indispensable to Paine, but it put him in a position of considerable importance. The work of the committee was almost experimental, since the relations of the infant republic to the rest of the world were not established. Its members were uncertain of themselves and of each other, while the fortunes of war soon made it difficult for them to be assembled. Thus the secretary, through whom communications ran, was very much in the center of political affairs. If he proved his ability, he might well expect to find his way into the ranks of statesmen. Less than three years earlier Paine had embarked for America unknown and penniless.

A few months after his appointment, in October, 1777, Paine's political importance was increased by the Pennsylvania Assembly, which engaged him to act as observer with Washington's army and report upon what it was doing. This also involved a salary, and it put him in a position to represent Washington's views to the Assembly. In this respect, however, the appointment did little more than confirm Paine in a position which he had taken up already.

A month previously, the British had outmaneuvered Washington at Brandywine Creek; and though he extricated his army, Philadelphia was threatened. Panic ensued; and Paine's fourth *Crisis* paper, which was published on September 13, was a short exhortation to the troops, to raise morale. On the 18th, Paine went to the speaker of the Assembly, Colonel Bayard, with a plan to save Philadelphia, asking for a voluntary assessment of $50,000 and three thousand volunteers to be mustered under General Thomas Mifflin. A resolute show of force, he reasoned, would be sufficient to hold Howe off until Washington could bring assistance.

Whether or not this was a practical proposal, General Mifflin paid no attention to it. He abandoned the city, and the British crossed the Schuylkill on the following morning, a beautiful sunlit day, Paine later recalled, with the streets "as full of men, women and children as on a market day." Paine was busy sending his personal belongings and all the papers of the Committee for Foreign

Affairs by boat to Trenton. He set out himself to join the army, but did not come up with it until the third of October because he did not dare to ask directions, not knowing Tory from patriot in the countryside. He found it starting out to march on Germantown, whither he followed at five the next morning.

Washington's raid on Germantown, at first successful, soon turned into a retreat which left Philadelphia firmly in British hands. Congress, meanwhile, retired to Lancaster and later to York. So many members had gone home that only about fifteen were usually present. The Committee for Foreign Affairs did not meet often and made few demands on Paine's time. He spent a good deal of the winter at Valley Forge with the army or with his friend, Colonel Joseph Kirkbride, at Bordentown, New Jersey. In February and March of 1778, he moved to Lancaster, Pennsylvania, to the house of William Henry, who was treasurer of the borough and shared with Paine an interest in science. Together they discussed some of the problems involved in applying steam power to boats, an idea which had occurred independently to both. But despite the interests which they had in common, Paine's habits were somewhat of a shock to his host.

He was at work at the time on his fifth *Crisis,* an important paper because it was written at the low point of the war when Washington's army was suffering extreme privation and the Congress had been driven out of Philadelphia. But Paine was in no hurry. He got up fairly late and went out for a walk, returning about noon for a midday meal which he managed to stretch, with conversation, till well after two o'clock. "He would then retire to his bed-chamber, wrap a blanket around him, and in a large arm chair take a nap, of two or three hours—rise and walk."

It is only fair to say that Paine's walks may well have helped him arrange his thoughts; but the Henry family contrasted his indolence with the virtues of Dr. David Rittenhouse, who was also a guest. "While that excellent man was employing his hours in the duties of his office . . . Paine would be a snoring away his precious time in his easy chair. . . . His remissness . . . caused great heart-burning among many primary characters in those days . . . His *Crisis,* No. V, lay on his table, dusted; today three or four lines would be added, in the course of a week, a dozen more, and so on."

These remarks, made many years later by Henry's son, who disapproved of Paine, must surely exaggerate the slowness of his output, since *Crisis* V was actually finished in March. In addition to some abuse of General Howe, it contains a review of the progress of the war highly favorable to Washington. Paine rejoices, of course, in the victories at Bennington and Saratoga; but these successes of Gates are nowhere contrasted with the failure of Washington to retake Philadelphia or to protect New Jersey. On the contrary, the affair of Germantown and the subsequent retreat of Howe to Philadelphia were represented almost as patriot successes. As for the British capture of Mud Island, which Paine had visited himself, he dismissed this as exhibiting the power of Britain in "a very contemptible light." Ignoring the strategic success won by Howe in clearing the mouth of the Delaware, he boasts that the garrison "were obliged to give it up more to the powers of time and gunpowder than to military superiority of the besiegers." One wonders what he thought military superiority was.

Paine's defense of Washington on this occasion was considerably less glowing than it had been in *Crisis* I, but it was even more timely. He knew that a movement was afoot to make the Gates, the victor of Saratoga, commander-in-chief. Years later and after a breach with Washington, Paine said that he realized the general's military blunders, but thought that only harm could come of dividing the army into factions.

In a time of crisis, Paine's mind was of a practical bent, so that he made constant suggestions for action. Some time during this winter he went to the Pennsylvania Navy Board with an offer to join up with four or five other people on an expedition downriver to set fire to the British fleet in the Delaware. In *Crisis* V, he worked out a recruiting scheme which amounted to a tax on every man of four dollars for paying bounties to army recruits, plus a system whereby wealthy men who were over age should supply blankets, cloaks, and shoes in lieu of personal service. We may note, however, that his practicality was always limited. Paine's habit with such schemes was merely to submit them for discussion, and he usually left decision to others.

In June, 1778, peace proposals brought by British commissioners produced a resounding scandal when George Johnstone, one of the commission, attempted to bribe various members of Congress. Paine published some satirical verses on the subject, calling Johnstone, who was once governor of Florida, "a turn coat patriot conquer'd by a jobb"; and he called for the exposure of the anonymous "lady" who had conveyed Johnstone's offer of ten thousand guineas to Joseph Reed, a member of Congress from

Philadelphia. These, and indeed other short articles were called forth by the emergencies of the moment; but the next two *Crisis* papers did not appear until the fall, by which time the British commissioners, recognizing their failure to treat with Congress, had published a direct appeal to the American people.

It was natural that "Common Sense" should reply to them. *Crisis* VI and VII, addressed to the American and the English people respectively, appeared three weeks apart. They have nothing essentially new to say. The American case is presented; the British ministry and king are abused. The American people, the British people, and even the Parliament are asked to look on the struggle in rational terms. No advantage can come to Britain from prolonging it, since American independence is sure and certain. "Perhaps it may be said," he writes to the British, "that I live in America and write this from interest. To this I reply, that my principle is universal. My attachment is to all the world, and not to any particular part." It was a large claim, yet not unfounded, as Paine's career was later to prove. Only for the present was this citizen of the world looking at America; yet while he did so, his influence there was unrivaled. The unity of the colonies in face of British offers was not a little owing to Paine's *Crisis* papers.

1778

The Great Deane Scandal

As long as "Common Sense" confined himself to appealing to the American people, or even to the British, his role as the mentor of the Revolution was assured; but the times were too crowded with incidents which held importance for the future. Constitutions were being shaped and parties formed. In dispute over such issues Paine was always at a disadvantage, simply because he had no roots in the country. His personal influence might be enormous; but he brought with him no organized body of opinion, no party, no votes. If he made enemies, no one was committed to defending him through thick and thin. Yet Paine was too large-minded a man to be content with asserting a bare independence from Great Britain. It was the American experiment which appealed to him, the chance to create a new government on principles of justice. He was bound to take sides because in his view these issues were vital. His first chance to do so arose in 1778 about the question of the constitution of Pennsylvania.

As we have seen, Paine had no share in framing this constitution, but its architect was Benjamin Franklin, his friend and patron. Its provisions were for the times exceedingly democratic, so that they have been much admired by some later writers. The fact was, however, that they threw power into the hands of a radical group of small farmers and artisans, many not of English descent and committed to a social as well as a political revolution. The well-to-do, be they Tory, Quaker, or Republican, perceived themselves threatened.

The aggressive nature of the radical group was expressed in an ordinance requiring an oath of loyalty to the new constitution. Since its provisions could not be amended for seven years, and then only at the discretion of a council of Censors which the party in power might hope to control, this seemed to the moderates like signing away their rights indefinitely. Battle was joined; and the state, already divided by the Tory leanings of the wealthy Quakers, was rent asunder.

In this controversy, Paine hastened to use the influence of "Common Sense" on the radical side. It was dangerous, he pointed out, to tamper with a constitution in time of war. Besides, if this one favored the poor, that in itself was an advantage to the rich, since consumers must be the basis of true prosperity. In the perfect state, there would be no discord between the interests of different classes; but as things now stood in the world, an ideal society could only be set up by raising the standards of the poor.

These general views might be true enough, and certainly they did Paine credit. They had little, however, to do with the practical problems of controlling inflation, destroying the power of the descendants of William Penn, or remaking the University in a new, more radical image. In other words, Paine was supporting a party whose program he had not helped to shape and possibly would not in every respect approve of.

While Paine was thus immersed in party politics, a scandal burst which soon tore both state and Congress asunder.

What was more, it was the direct concern of the Secretary to the Committee for Foreign Affairs, since it involved the questions of the treaty with France and the scope of French aid to America.

At the time of the outbreak of war in 1775, an irregular army, rapidly assembled out of volunteers, was equipped with muskets and powder collected from house to house throughout the countryside. The supply of both was quite inadequate; indeed, it has been suggested there was not enough powder in the thirteen colonies to last for a single week of serious fighting. We have seen how Thomas Paine tried to work out a method of producing gunpowder in private households. Even if this had been successful, however, it could never have supplied the rifles, blankets, cannon, shoes, or money needed to keep an army in the field. In fact, the resources of the colonies by themselves were not equal to the struggle.

The necessity of help from abroad was seen by all the colonial leaders. The Congress not merely established a committee to correspond with friends of the colonies but, despite its financial difficulties, made appropriations for the expenses of foreign agents. Meanwhile Arthur Lee, brother of two prominent Virginia statesmen and agent for the colonies in London, was studying the state of affairs in France in the hope of persuading its government to help. He happened recently to have been in contact with a fascinating Frenchman of many talents.

Caron de Beaumarchais, born in 1732, was the son of a jeweler and had invented an improvement in watches at the age of twenty which brought him in a modest fortune. He used it to buy an office at court, "Controller of the Pantry of the King's Household." It became his duty to march in with the royal dinner procession, hand some dishes, and stand by looking important with a sword at his side. Presently he married a wealthy widow and bought another office, Secretary to the King, which entailed no work but carried with it a patent of nobility. In other words, M. de Beaumarchais was now a gentleman. He set himself up as a literary man and wrote a comedy, *Le Barbier de Seville,* which became an instant success and a French classic. Dabbling in one thing after another, he speculated, studied some law, and visited England, where he discussed American affairs with Arthur Lee. There was enthusiastic talk between them about France furnishing five million livres to the American cause. Presently Beaumarchais returned to Paris and presented a memoir to King Louis XVI in which he predicted that the colonies would triumph and argued that they therefore should be supported.

The suggestion was attractive, but Louis was aware that his treaty with England would not permit him to lend open aid to her rebellious subjects. In the present financial condition of France, he could not afford to be drawn into a war with Great Britain. He hesitated. In the meantime Arthur Lee, too much of a politician to let slip a chance to gain credit, was writing to Congress that his own pressure on the French minister in London had resulted in Beaumarchais' being secretly sent to offer him French supplies. In the hopes of making this come true, he was pointing out to the French that if they refused their assistance, they would make themselves the laughingstock of Europe.

No doubt the progress of the affair was confusing to Congress, several months behind events in Europe. It was obvious in any case that if France were to grant aid, an envoy would have to go over to manage the business. Arthur Lee, more or less on the spot, might possibly have done; and there is no doubt that he would have liked the appointment. But either because the Lees and their radical faction had not yet come to their full strength in Congress, or because it seemed better to send someone who could be instructed more carefully at home, Congress selected Silas Deane, a Connecticut statesman whose business abilities had made a good impression.

Silas Deane's appointment was dated March, 1776, before the Declaration of Independence, yet after the publication of *Common Sense*. He was not at present the agent of an independent nation, but it was obvious that he would shortly become so. The colonies, therefore, would like to know if France would recognize their independence if they were to declare it. They would then like to send a minister openly and make a treaty of alliance. In the meantime, they needed clothing and arms for twenty-five thousand, plus ammunition and a hundred cannon.

Deane's pay was to depend on his success and was calculated on a percentage of the value of the goods he obtained from France. It stood to reason that he could not receive this until after considerable delay, but it was understood that his position would also enable him to make a fair fortune out of private trade.

Robert Morris, head of the great mercantile firm of Willing and Morris, was eager at this time to put his vast resources at the disposal of the government. Indeed, it was highly necessary that he should do so, since the colonies had no adequate banking system. Morris' money, however, was tied up in England so that he could not get at it. He needed to transfer assets to France, which was only possible if he could raise loans there and embark on trade.

It suited him well to employ Deane as his agent because an official envoy, even if on secret business, suggested that the government would back him. In this way Morris was using the credit of Congress, while Congress in turn was using the credit of Morris.

After this irregular fashion Deane acquired two functions, that of Morris' agent and that of buyer for the Congress. He exchanged these hats with bewildering rapidity, while at the same time he was trading on his own. Small wonder that his accounts proved difficult to disentangle.

Meanwhile, complications mounted in France. Beaumarchais had persuaded the king that the best way to cover up what France was doing was to form a private company to which the French government would secretly hand over a large sum of money. This could be used to purchase weapons from French government arsenals, which were overflowing with obsolete firearms from the recent war with England. These, then, could be sent to America.

The King of France duly gave a million livres, and his relative, the King of Spain, gave another million. These sums were turned over to Hortalez and Co., which was the firm which Beaumarchais had created for the purpose. Supplies took time to collect and more time to ship, but eventually they began to flow across the Atlantic and were responsible in large measure for General Gates's victory at Saratoga.

So far so good; but how was Hortalez and Co. to be repaid? Beaumarchais expected to make a fortune from commissions, so that he had invested his private resources in the affair, together with every sou that he could borrow. Meanwhile, Deane's letters of instruction from Congress had been few; and his requests for Virginia tobacco, salt fish, and other colonial goods in payment were ignored.

Congress, the width of the Atlantic away, was confused by the whole transaction. Arthur Lee was furious at the appointment of Deane and, no doubt to show how well he could have handled the affair, was reporting on it. His impression certainly was that the two million livres advanced to Hortalez had been a gift from the French and Spanish nations to the rebellious colonies. Whether this in fact was so has been debated from that day to this. The inefficiency of the French government was so great that the transaction may have been viewed in different ways by Louis and his ministers. In any event, Beaumarchais varied his story with his mood and could not be trusted to write two letters to Congress which agreed with one another. However, his general idea appears to have been that the Americans would pay in tobacco, from the profits of which he would take his own commission. He would expend the rest on fresh goods to send over, and be paid in more tobacco. In other words, the original gift to him was in the nature of seed money to start trade on an ever-increasing scale.

Congress listened to Arthur Lee and made no payments, so that Beaumarchais was driven gradually closer to ruin. Frantically he put pressure on Deane, who wrote urgently to Congress. Lee's brothers in Congress, notably Richard Henry Lee, head of the Committee for Foreign Affairs to which Paine was secretary, accused Beaumarchais and Deane of demanding repayment of the kings' gift with the intention of putting the money into their own pockets.

While this situation was still developing, the Declaration of Independence was published. It now became possible for the new nation to seek recognition and alliance openly from France. This seemed too much for Deane to handle alone, since he was entangled in the munitions traffic. Besides, it was necessary to push American interests in Holland, Spain, and other countries more or less dependent on France. Congress therefore appointed three commissioners, Lee, Deane, and Benjamin Franklin, to negotiate a treaty with France and extract further supplies. As it turned out, Franklin took over the diplomatic negotiations and Lee the situation in Holland and elsewhere, leaving Deane with the business he was conducting already. From this time on, however, all three commissioners were jointly responsible for what he did.

Arthur Lee, by nature jealous and headstrong, was soon convinced that Deane was dishonest. He could not make head or tail of the confusion between Deane's private accounts, those of Willing and Morris, and the records of Deane's official business. Lee also disliked Deane and thought he was living suspiciously beyond his means.

It has never been proved that Deane was embezzling public funds, but Lee was right about his weakness of character. Deane was in contact with more than one British agent who engaged him in dubious schemes. In fact, we now know that he joined in sending news to England of the secret treaty between America and France, planning to make a speculative fortune out of its effect on the British stock exchange. The conflicts of personal and public interest were presenting many new problems to the inexperienced nation, but Deane had been drawn into actions which could not be excused.

Lee's suspicions of his colleague soon led to wrangling among the three commissioners to France. Franklin perceived no objection to private trade and had allowed his great-nephew to enter Deane's employment. He could not see that Lee had discovered evidence to support his charges. Deane's services had been considerable. His contribution to the Saratoga victory, for instance, had been expressed in shoes, blankets, stockings, cannon, gun carriages, fusils, musket balls, flints, gun worms, cannon balls, lead, gunpowder, mortars, bombs, grapeshot, hand grenades, spades, shovels, axes, tents, and sulphur. Moreover, when the money of Hortalez and Co. had been exhausted, he had extracted further credit from the French. Franklin supported Deane and was in consequence accused by Lee of sharing in the profit of his dealings.

Congress, divided into factions on the issue, recalled Deane to report. Unluckily for himself, the terms of his summons did not convey to him that he would have to answer charges. It was in any case unwise to entrust the details of his accounts to a ship which might be captured. Thus when he returned at the end of the summer of 1778, he had nothing with him but a brief statement of what he had bought on his country's behalf and what was owing.

By the time that Deane reported to Congress on the 15th of August, his case was only part of a larger quarrel. The vast question of public versus private interests involved particularly the financial empires of men like Robert Morris, who had agents everywhere. A number of grievances which were being felt in America had focussed interest on Morris' affairs and those of other wealthy merchants. In Pennsylvania, the dispute over the constitution had enraged radical leaders against them. Inflation, pressing hardest on the poorer classes, was arousing fury against war profiteers throughout the country. Thus to many politicians Deane was chiefly important because he had been Robert Morris' agent.

The result of this situation was that when Deane pressed for a hearing in order to vindicate himself before Congress, he was not granted it. Richard Henry Lee and Henry Laurens, at that time President of Congress, were after bigger game. It did not suit them to have Deane defend himself until an investigation of all the proceedings of all three commissioners and their connections had taken place.

Frustrated and unpaid, Deane was not the man to keep silent. On December 5, he wrote an open letter to the people, charging that Congress had refused to hear his defense. It was printed in the *Pennsylvania Packet* and widely circulated in handbills at Deane's expense. In it he exposed Congress as being too deeply divided by faction to judge his case on its merits. The revelation was comforting to the enemies of the young republic and disconcerting to its friends; it was also highly offensive to Congress.

It was at this point in the affair that Paine took a hand. As secretary to the Committee for Foreign Affairs he was suspicious of Deane's conduct in France; as patriot and radical he wished to protect the poor against inflation and was concerned about the war profiteering of Robert Morris. He was intimate with Henry Laurens and Richard Henry Lee. He cared deeply for the reputation of Congress. Accordingly, he attacked Deane in a series of newspaper letters for his indiscretion in making confidential affairs public. At the same time he privately urged Laurens to investigate Deane's connections with Robert Morris.

Paine's motives in the matter seem creditable, but he

soon proved that he was as indiscreet as Deane. In his fourth article on the subject he asserted that the supplies sent over had been promised by the French as a present before Deane ever arrived in Europe. This was information he could only have got from his secretaryship, though in taking up this office he had sworn to keep official secrets.

Paine's own view was that Britain knew perfectly well how France had behaved, that an alliance had by now been openly signed between America and France, and that France had come to a breach with England. Thus he did not regard the earlier agreement as being secret any longer.

The Chevalier de Gérard, French minister to the United States, took the opposite view. He was on good personal terms with Deane, whom he had known well in France. They had sailed for America on the same ship and had been cooped up together for the length of the voyage. In any case, it did not accord with the honor of France that she should admit to having given assistance to rebels within the territories of an ally before any question had arisen of the colonies being independent. Thomas Paine in his naïveté had not reckoned with the fact that the honor of nations will permit them to do things which must not be talked about.

Gérard went swiftly into action. At first he attempted to get Paine to withdraw his statement. Shortly after arriving in America, Gérard had seen the importance of Paine as a propagandist and had heard about his insufficient income. He had approached him, offering payment for a series of pro-French articles, which he pointed out Paine might suitably produce now that an alliance had been signed between the two nations. Paine had seen the trap and refused to become a French agent, but his relations with Gérard were still cordial. The influence of Lee and Laurens over him, however, prevented him from retracting his article. Gérard therefore protested to Congress that M. de Beaumarchais had been a private agent, so that Paine's revelations had been untrue as well as indiscreet.

Considering the importance of France to the American cause, it is not surprising that Congress was angry with Paine. He was called before the bar of the House, not permitted to say a word in his own defense, but merely asked whether he had written the article to which Gérard objected. A hectic debate followed in which Paine's enemies attacked him for five days. Paine petitioned to be heard in his own defense, but was refused. He resigned his office, while the Congress officially disavowed his revelation, unblushingly stating that His Most Christian Majesty, the King of France, had not sent any supplies to America before the time of the alliance.

So unpopular was Paine with the conservative party at this time that anger erupted into violence. A certain Matthew Slough, one of Morris' agents, who had been drinking with his friends, was going home down Market Street when Paine met them.

"There comes Common Sense," said one of the company.

"Damn him," replied Slough. "I shall common sense him." He took the wall, leaving Paine to pass on the street side of the pavement. As they went by, Slough tripped him and threw him on his back into the gutter, "which at that time was very offensive and filthy."

This was unpleasant enough; but what was far worse was that Paine, who had hoped he was going to make his mark as a statesman, was forced back to the position of outsider. This rebuff was fatal to his future in American politics.

The victor in the situation so far was clearly Gérard; but, aware of Paine's vast reputation, the French Minister was anxious to prevent him from saying more. Several times he offered money through agents, which was refused. Then, making a final effort, he invited him to dinner. Paine, who understood that his reputation would be ruined if he allowed himself to be muzzled now, succeeded through the evening in turning the talk into harmless channels. Gérard, however, was not to be put off. As his guest rose to go, he said to him directly: "Mr. Paine, I have always had a great respect for you, and should be glad of the opportunity of showing you more solid marks of my friendship."

The upshot was that Paine refused any money and persisted in the controversy, actually quoting correspondence from Franklin, Deane, and Lee with his Committee in support of what he had already made public.

By this time Paine thought of himself as an innocent victim of the friends of Deane. He was bound to pursue the quarrel for his own sake, while in addition he was truly concerned about the war profiteering which was a current scandal in Philadelphia. He turned a suspicious eye on Robert Morris, who was hand in glove with a certain John Holker, French Consul-General at Philadelphia, with whom he was involved in purchasing supplies for the French navy. Paine suspected that Holker, by paying black-market prices through Morris, was swelling the merchant's profits and pushing up prices.

In May, 1779, a vessel called the *Victorious* arrived in Philadelphia. Robert Morris, who was handling the cargo, was so alarmed by the state of public opinion that he had the ship put under guard. This in turn gave rise to rumors that it belonged to Deane and that Congress was detaining it until Deane's accounts were examined. A general meeting of citizens was called, and resolutions were put through demanding the investigation of Deane and Morris. A committee was chosen to look into the matter, to which Paine was appointed. Morris, as it turned out, was merely managing the cargo for a merchant of Baltimore; but his statement that he had insisted the goods be sold for a reasonable price was widely doubted.

Further attacks on Morris and Holker made by Paine and his watchdog committee produced another protest to Congress from Gérard, the French minister. Philadelphia retorted with another general town meeting, at which indignation rose so high that Morris' supporters withdrew to form a meeting of their own. Paine, whose articles in the public press had kept the controversy alive, was voted a friend to the American cause by the majority group. A few days later he was elected to a second committee for regulating prices in Philadelphia.

This second complaint of Gérard's was answered by a letter in which John Jay, now President of Congress, supported the French and condemned the Philadelphia committee. The Council of Pennsylvania, led by Paine's friend Timothy Matlack, replied by a resolution recommending that Holker employ "fair and unsuspected persons" in his further purchases.

Such an insult infuriated Morris' and Holker's chief purchasing agent, a merchant named Jonathan Rumford, who was not without friends. The dispute went merrily on, Deane, Holker and Morris being ranged on the conservative side, while the opposition was led by Paine and the Lees, together with Timothy Matlack, leader of the radical side in Pennsylvania. As more people were drawn into the conflict, it once again widened its scope.

Ever since the interference of Gérard in the dispute, there had been an anti-French bias among the opponents of Deane. This is not to say that Paine himself was anti-French, but he was at least pro-American. At this time America and France were discussing together the terms of an acceptable peace; and French interests were not in favor of prolonging the war at vast expense where France herself had little to gain. American independence was the common concern of both, but fishing rights off Nova Scotia were a purely American issue. In the middle of 1779, articles signed "Americanus" appeared in the *Pennsylvania Gazette* arguing the French case, which was that these rights need not be abandoned but should not be included in a peace treaty. If they were to be so, they would certainly prolong the war.

Paine immediately took up the cudgels, pointing out that French interests did not in this case coincide with American ones. He strongly suspected that "Americanus" was the New York politician Gouverneur Morris, friend though not relative of Robert Morris.

This particular incident had further importance for Paine's future. Gouverneur Morris, though he denied the authorship, can hardly have relished Paine's attack. Besides, the two were in every way opposite. Gouverneur

Morris was young, athletic, handsome, aristocratic, and a great ladies' man. He had the head for business which Paine lacked, as well as the instinct for practical politics. Never interested in theory, he despised Paine's abilities almost as thoroughly as he did his failings. To him, Paine was a man whose lack of family, education, polished manners, or roots in the country made him unfit to be trusted. He was an upstart, and such people were by nature unscrupulous. Everything that Paine had done in the great Deane controversy had served to confirm Morris in a dislike which was personal and instinctive as well as political.

It happened that a further turn of events had put Paine in a dubious light. Like many conversationalists, he was not always discreet in company; and he had boasted to a friend of his, Charles Willson Peale, the artist, that he had turned down an income of seven hundred dollars a year in order to preserve his independence. He did not mention that the offer came from Gérard, but this discretion only did him harm. Peale jumped to the conclusion that it was Deane who had attempted to bribe him. Enraged by newspaper attacks on Paine, he stated publicly what he believed. Deane responded by demanding details which could not, of course, be supplied. Paine did not like to retract, and yet he could hardly persist in a false accusation. He answered that he had given particulars of the offer to Congress and would do so again if asked, but that he could not reveal them to the public.

The great Deane controversy wore itself out in the end. Chief losers by it were Beaumarchais and Deane. The unfortunate Frenchman got no answers to his increasingly frantic demands for repayment. He was forced to go bankrupt, and even though Alexander Hamilton in 1793 agreed that at least $2,280,000 was due him—and possibly a million more—he was allowed to starve in a garret in Hamburg. Thirty years later his daughter, after pressing her claim for eleven years, was finally paid off at twenty-five cents on the dollar.

Despite more than forty appeals to Congress, Deane never got a hearing. Eventually, assured that Congress would appoint an auditor of his accounts, he went back to France at his own expense and spent a year there disentangling his affairs with the help of a paid clerk. But when an auditor was appointed to look into the whole question of French loans and American payments, it turned out that his instructions did not cover Deane's transactions. By 1781, Deane was completely ruined and Paris was too expensive for him. He moved to Antwerp, whence he once more got in touch with the British. George III wrote to his minister, Lord North, "I think it perfectly right that Mr. Deane should be so far trusted as to have £3,000 in goods for America." It was possible, he thought, that Deane might persuade one of the provinces to return to its allegiance to England.

Deane was not inclined to put himself in danger on the American continent, but he had to deliver something for his money. He wrote a number of pro-British letters to influential American friends and sent them to Lord North for his approval. From him they went to Sir Henry Clinton in America with the statement that they had "fallen into" North's hands and that Clinton might possibly see fit to publish them.

It is difficult to see what advantage North or Clinton

might expect from making public what had been designed as private offers. Clinton, however, did publish in the *Royal Gazette* five days after Cornwallis' surrender at Yorktown. The American victory disposed of any question, if there ever had been one, of Deane's corrupting anybody. All the letters did was vindicate Paine, since even Deane's supporters agreed that so base a man must have been guilty of all he had been accused of. It is true that two years later a commission did admit that Deane's expenses and his five-per-cent commission were actually owing. No action, however, was taken till 1842, at which time Congress gave Deane's heirs $37,000, graciously explaining that the former audit was "ex parte, erroneous, and a gross injustice to Silas Deane."

Another loser in the affair was Thomas Paine. He had, as we have seen, resigned the official position, which for him had really been a toe in the door. He had lost friends, too. Benjamin Franklin had been attacked together with Deane. The Baches, Franklin's daughter and son-in-law, who had been so kind to Paine on his arrival, were violently against him now. As Sarah Bache wrote to her father, "There never was a man less beloved in a place than Paine is in this, having at different times disputed with everybody. The most rational thing he could have done would have been to have died the instant he had finished his *Common Sense,* for he never again will have it in his power to leave the world with such credit." Truth was, Paine had become a party man; and this position was particularly dangerous for him because he was in fact above party and quite capable of changing sides over a matter of principle. Such anger did he arouse that it is difficult from this time on to do his character justice because it has been so unscrupulously blackened. Yet Paine was still the watchdog of the people, among whom the influence of *Common Sense* had scarcely diminished.

1779-83

Later Years of the War

Paine's resignation from the Committee for Foreign Affairs left him without income, and for a year he had to support himself by working at a common clerk's wages for Owen Biddle, a Philadelphia merchant. This coincided with the time when he was so active on committees; and in the circumstances, his poverty rankled.

"I think I have a right to a horse of my own," he wrote to Henry Laurens, "but I cannot even afford to hire one, which is a situation I never was in before."

He was right in thinking that it was a waste of his time to trudge about on foot, but his position was peculiar. Independence was absolutely necessary to him. Unless it was understood that the opinions of "Common Sense" were not to be bought, he might spare himself the trouble of having any. If he had been a party man, it might have been possible to be paid for setting out what all knew was his position. But Paine's strength and weakness was that his convictions were too individual to be directed by party policy. Thus pay from anyone looked most suspiciously like bribery.

Another difficulty was that Paine's efforts to make a living were irregular and unsystematic. In practical affairs, he was always that kind of man. In any case, however, his sense of his own value to the cause was great, while his burning conviction was that the birth of the United States was the most important event which had occurred since the Creation. Governments hitherto had produced more misery than good because they had rested on force and had served the interests of the few rather than the many. He saw the dawn of a new age, and he simply could not keep his mind on his own affairs while he had chances to help mankind in making a fresh start. In fact, no sooner did he begin to earn than he would find his services needed, throw up his work, and plunge into political activity which lasted until his funds ran out. By such efforts, he produced some notable writing as well as various practical schemes for the public good. But constant changes of direction did not endear him to those who dealt with him. His position became more precarious, not less, as the war went on.

Paine's first idea on making money was to bring out a special edition of *Common Sense* and his *Crisis* papers, to be paid for by public subscription. Nothing came of this, and he turned to Gérard for help in preparing a history of the war. His relations with the French minister were still polite on the surface, but Gérard's real opinion of him was expressed to the President of the Executive Council of Pennsylvania when Paine applied for a literary pension to enable him to continue public work.

"If you believe you are able to guide his pen for public welfare and utility," wrote Gérard, "which perhaps will not be difficult for your zeal, your talent, and your superior enlightenment, I shall be the first to applaud the success of an attempt in which I have failed."

It need hardly be said that Paine received no pension. Luckily, however, his Pennsylvania friends were in power, so that he was shortly appointed clerk to the Pennsylvania Assembly, in which capacity he was able to register one decree which had his whole-hearted support, namely, a bill for the abolition of slavery. Tradition says that the eloquent preamble to this bill was written by Paine.

His new position once more put Paine in direct touch with events. The British had turned south, and the conquest of Georgia by the end of 1779 was followed by the threat to South Carolina. By May, 1780, General Washington took a gloomy view, which he expressed in a confidential letter which Paine read to the Assembly behind closed doors. The army was destitute and likely to dissolve through wholesale desertion.

Such an appeal brought out the best in Paine. Inflation might be rampant, taxes inadequate, and public credit exhausted; but individuals must come to the rescue. Immediately he drew all the salary owing to him and wrote a letter to a prominent merchant he knew, proposing a voluntary subscription to offer bounties for recruits and enclosing five hundred dollars, which was half of all he possessed.

The idea caught on. Robert Morris and other financiers were interested in the scheme; and the subscription developed into the Bank of North America, which supplied credit to the army for the rest of the war. In his desire to be of service, Paine had crossed party lines to cooperate with the very men who had been for the last year or more his principal targets.

Almost immediately after Washington's letter came the disastrous news of the surrender of Charleston. To raise men's spirits, Paine published a ninth *Crisis,* which was followed not long after by another which, lifting a phrase from one of Washington's letters, he labeled *The Crisis Extraordinary*. Taxes in England, he pointed out, drawing heavily on his experience as an excise officer, are far higher than those in America. Were England to win the war, her first act would be to impose drastic levies. It is thus to the interest of every citizen to resist. On the other hand, it is true that American taxes are not high enough at the moment. They need never equal the British, but they ought to take care of the cost of the war. It would actually be cheaper to pay sufficient now than to prolong the fighting at ruinous cost in lives and property. Paine proceeded to recommend new excise taxes.

"It would be a satisfaction to me was there a duty on all sorts of liquors during the war, as in my idea of things it would be an addition to the pleasures of society to know, that when the health of the army goes round, a few drops from every glass becomes theirs."

Paine had not been satisfied with merely toasting the army. A month before *The Crisis Extraordinary* was published, he had proposed that he go on a secret mission to England. His scheme was to pretend to be an Englishman who had made a tour of America incognito. In this guise he would publish articles in the press which, he flattered himself, would open the eyes of the British public.

Nobody who knew what Paine was capable of could fail to hope that this plan might be effective. In preparation for a secret departure, Paine submitted his resignation as Clerk of the Assembly, under the pretense of devoting time to his history. It was pointed out, however, that he might find himself in great danger. The recent treachery of Benedict Arnold had been followed by the execution of Major André as a spy. The British would be eager to lay hands on anyone of Paine's importance in retaliation. They might hang, draw, and quarter him for treason, rather than shoot him.

There was no point in inviting martyrdom, and the only result of the affair was that Paine was again without an income. He was forced to approach the French once more. Perhaps there were services which he could properly render for pay. The Chevalier de La Luzerne, who had succeeded Gérard, went so far as to consider sponsoring the history which Paine was never to bring out. But Paine was probably tided over this period by the following commission from a private company.

Paine had suggested in *Common Sense* that the back lands of America could be sold as a means of paying for the war. The idea had been taken up in Congress, but the State of Virginia laid claim to most of them and had actually set up an office to sell them. Concerned as he was about the issue, Paine felt unwilling to press the matter, lest he provoke dissension at a crucial time. He was intimate, moreover, with the Lees and other Virginians, so that he declined to be on a commission for settling boundaries between Pennsylvania and Virginia.

In 1779, Paine was approached by the Indiana Company, which had bought a large tract from the Indians now claimed by the State of Virginia. He refused to take up their case, regarding himself as above becoming a company agent. A year later, however, the Indiana Company produced documents which demolished the entire Virginia claim. Paine consented to use these, provided he need not mention the company in a discussion of the whole subject.

The grateful company voted Paine twelve thousand acres of land, which he thought of so little importance that he neglected to apply for a deed. It appears, however, that they also gave him money. His publication, a sound piece of historical reasoning, raised fury against him in Virginia, adding to the list of his enemies, which was already too long for comfort. Soon afterward his acceptance of a reward came out and was made a basis for attacks on his reputation. Paine's conscience was easy on the matter, since he had merely taken up a cause on which he had already expressed his opinion. All the same, the outcry was uncomfortable to him and warned him to be careful in the future.

His next project for keeping his head above water was to found a newspaper of his own. He had not got further than buying a quantity of paper when another chance to be of service arose. Partly as a result of *The Crisis Extraordinary,* certain members of Congress thought it possible that some of the money needed at once for the war might be procured from France. Colonel John Laurens, son of the ex-President of Congress, was therefore appointed Envoy Extraordinary to go and ask for it. He besought Paine to go with him as secretary, insisting that he was not experienced enough to undertake the mission without Paine's advice. Paine's enemies in Congress objected violently to his appointment, so that eventually the matter had to be settled by his accompanying Laurens at his own expense.

They sailed on the frigate *Alliance* in February, 1781. Paine was seldom lucky in his ocean voyages, and this one proved no exception. They had a turbulent crew, drafted partly from British prisoners; they ran through icebergs and were nearly wrecked; they released a merchantman captured by a Scottish cutter; and Paine got the itch, a not uncommon shipboard complaint.

They landed at L'Orient and rode up to Nantes, where

they lodged with Elkanah Watson of Philadelphia. The Mayor and other distinguished citizens called to pay their respects to "Common Sense"; and Watson, who was employed to interpret, says he was mortified at Paine's filthy appearance and unseemly address. Besides, as he had been "roasted alive" for the itch in L'Orient and "well basted with brimstone, he was absolutely offensive and perfumed the whole apartment."

Paine, whose baggage seemed not yet to have arrived, asked to borrow a clean shirt. Watson insisted that he must first have a bath. To his indignation, Paine refused to consider bathing until he was offered a file of the English papers to look over while soaking himself.

Thus says Elkanah Watson, adding: "He was coarse and uncouth in his manners, loathsome in his appearance, and a disgusting egotist, rejoicing most in talking of himself, and reading the effusions of his own mind."

At precisely this same time, Franklin's great-nephew Jonathan Williams, who accompanied Paine to Nantes, was writing to Franklin: "I confess I like him as a companion because he is a pleasant as well as a sensible man."

No amount of juggling can reconcile these two descriptions of Paine. We have to believe one or the other. It is interesting, therefore, to see that he kept the affections of Laurens. The business which brought Laurens to France was speedily transacted with Franklin's experienced aid. The king granted six million livres as a present, plus a further ten as a loan. Paine was flattered by his own reputation in France and delighted by the kindness of Benjamin Franklin, who bore him no personal malice for the Deane affair. He even considered whether he would not be more useful to the Revolution in Europe, where he might explain the American cause to the French people. Laurens, however, put pressure on him to return for friendship's sake, pointing out that their responsibility was by no means over.

They landed in Boston on August 25 with two and a half million livres in silver for immediate needs. This was transported by sixteen ox teams to the bank at Philadelphia. Laurens, who was remaining in Providence on business, found himself short of cash; but he was forced to divide what he had with Paine, who had spent all his savings. Out of the six guineas thus obtained, Paine paid his own expenses home and those of a servant of Laurens' who traveled with him. When he arrived at Bordentown, New Jersey, he was destitute and had to borrow a dollar to cross on the ferry.

Robert Morris, now Superintendent of Finance, was above bearing malice for Paine's persecution of him earlier. Their cooperation in founding the Bank of North America had brought them together, while *The Crisis Extraordinary* had been of real assistance to those who were trying to stabilize the country's finances. The French money brought back by Laurens and Paine had been desperately needed to stave off bankruptcy. Altogether, Morris owed a good deal to Paine and thought that he might find some way to use his talents.

Paine, meanwhile, had applied for help to Washington. After all he had done to keep up morale, raise funds for the army, and increase Washington's own reputation, it was natural that the General should feel obliged. Accordingly he passed on to Morris a wish that something or other could be done for Paine.

The upshot of these negotiations was that Morris, Superintendent of Finance, Robert Livingston, Secretary for Foreign Affairs, and Washington, Commander-in-chief, signed an agreement to pay Paine eight hundred dollars a year out of a secret fund in return for his services. Paine was to urge the states to provide sufficient revenue for Congress and to enlarge its powers. He was to keep up morale and comment on military matters. Washington and Livingston were to furnish him with information as it was needed. The agreement was to be kept secret. Paine saw no objection to being paid for writing in this vein, but the affair of the Indiana Company had served as a warning that his motives might not be understood.

The first result of this agreement was *Crisis* X, which appeared in March, 1782. Though Paine cast his article in the form of an answer to George III's speech at the opening of Parliament, his real task was to urge that the states grant Congress sufficient funds and powers to win the war. Shortly afterward he wrote another piece on the same theme, inviting Washington and Morris to come to his lodgings for "a few oysters or a crust of bread and cheese," to talk it over.

Both these articles had been submitted to the French minister before they were published. There was no reason why they should not be, since the fullest cooperation existed between Paine's employers and La Luzerne. The consequence was that *Crisis* XI was actually paid for by the French. It is an attempt to prepare the American public for the fact that Britain, having in vain tried to negotiate a separate peace with France, Holland, and Spain, was likely to approach the United States. Pride, Paine cried indignantly, is insulted by the suggestion. "It is calling us villains, for no man asks the other to act the villain unless he believes him inclined to be one."

One connection with La Luzerne soon led to another. Paine's work on a history of the war, never quite abandoned, yet never vigorously tackled, had led to his reading a French work on the American Revolution by a certain Abbé Raynal. He was immediately aroused to answer. Raynal's thesis was that the dispute between the colonies and Britain had been over nothing wider than taxation. He added that peace would have been signed on the terms which Britain offered in 1778, had it not been for the French alliance. Thus the birth of the new nation became a side issue, and its success was due entirely to the French. These ideas were not acceptable to either La Luzerne or Paine. They laid the French ministry open to criticism for treating America as an equal ally; and at the same time, they encouraged England to lay all the blame for the war at France's door.

For reasons such as these, Paine's *Letter to the Abbé Raynal,* though printed at his own expense, had the blessing of La Luzerne, who gave Paine fifty guineas and hastened to send a copy to the French foreign minister. Paine himself hoped it would add to his European reputation, as indeed it did, being speedily translated into French and well received. La Luzerne, meanwhile, employed Paine to write *A Supernumary Crisis,* calling on the states to unite against British pressure to control their trade.

While Paine was writing for La Luzerne, his agreement with Livingston, Morris, and Washington was bearing fruit also. It was Livingston, for instance, who called his attention to the Asgill case. Captain Huddy of the Jersey militia had been taken prisoner by a group of Tories fighting on the British side, who had hanged him. Clinton, the American commander, demanded that the officer responsible be handed over as a murderer. Being refused, he selected Captain Asgill, a British officer in his hands, to be hanged in reprisal. Naturally there was a great outcry, and Paine was asked to defend the American position. He did so in *A Supernumary Crisis* addressed to Sir Guy Carleton, the British commander. Privately, however, he wrote to Washington, asking that Asgill's life be spared. Luckily Marie Antoinette was moved to do the same, so that it became possible to release him as a gracious gesture to the French queen.

The next emergency which arose concerned a five-percent import duty adopted by Congress to pay the interest on foreign and domestic loans. This measure had to be ratified by all the states, but Rhode Island was adamant against it. This was exactly the sort of issue covered by Paine's agreement. Accordingly, he wrote half a dozen articles for the Providence *Gazette* in December and January, 1782-83. He followed these with a personal visit to Rhode Island, but only managed to arouse indignation there. He was denounced as an agent of Congress meddling in state affairs; and though this was officially denied, it was near enough the truth to be believed by many. Once more it was obvious that Paine could only be effective as a private agent.

His own conscience about his methods of making a living was clear. His pen essentially was not for sale. In his thirteenth *Crisis,* dated April 19, 1783, on the eighth anniversary of the Battle of Lexington and Concord, he celebrates victory by stating his own view of what he has done in the last two years.

"I have avoided all places of profit or office, either in the state I live in, or in the United States; kept myself at a distance from all parties and party connections, and even disregarded all private and inferior concerns."

"But as the scenes of war are closed," he concludes, "and every man preparing for home and happier times, I therefore take my leave of the subject. I have most sincerely followed it from beginning to end, and through all its turns and windings: and whatever country I may hereafter be in, I shall always feel an honest pride at the part I have taken and acted, and a gratitude to nature and providence for putting it in my power to be of some use to mankind."

A citizen of the world can put his views no better. It is for others to build the new country. For his own part, Paine does not even know where he wants to live; and he prides himself not on his service to America, but his use to all mankind. It is a fitting farewell, but Paine was not quite done. *A Supernumary Crisis* at the end of the year once more calls for union to resist British pressure and promote freedom of trade. Essentially, however, with the peace his duties were over. Party politicians would carry on the struggle now, and national leaders would emerge from those who had a stake in the country. An exciting nine years had raised Paine to dizzy eminence, but had set him on the road to nowhere. Whither should he turn?

1783-87
Postwar Interlude

Paine's eloquent farewell in the *Thirteenth Crisis* had been written in the knowledge that his agreement with Morris, Washington, and Livingston was at an end. As usual, he was looking about for an income, inclining to projects which he later abandoned, took up again, and once more relinquished. He was seriously considering going to France in order to promote good feeling toward America there. Perhaps he was hoping for an official appointment in connection with the American Embassy in Paris; but if so, he was disappointed. Presently he decided he had better prospects at home.

On the advice of Morris, he drew up a letter to Congress reviving his old project of a history. No one, he pointed out, could be in a better position to write impartially about the war, seeing that he was free from state and party connections. All he needed was a substantial sum of money to support him while he tackled this great task.

The idea was a plausible one; and even those who knew Paine well enough to doubt his perseverance thought that his services deserved some reward. It was ridiculous that he should have made nothing out of the enormous sale of *Common Sense*. His *Crisis* papers had been timely, eloquent, and influential. Over and over again they had revived failing spirits, suggested new ways around difficulties, appealed over the heads of sectional interests to the country at large. If Paine had been a modern radio commentator, he must through such a career have grown rich. Even without anticipating the conditions of the twentieth century, Congress could see that something was owing to him from the nation. But though a committee reported favorably on the project, Paine's enemies were strong enough to block further discussion.

With the modest sum he had earned near the end of the war, Paine had bought himself a few acres and a house at Bordentown, New Jersey. It was close to his intimate friend Colonel Kirkbride and also convenient for attending Congress, which was then sitting in Princeton. Washington, who had taken up residence in an official mansion prepared for him nearby, asked him over for a few days, remarking that a visit to the President might remind Congress of how greatly all were indebted to "Common Sense."

An invitation such as this, expressed in the warmest terms, was not to be refused. Paine visited in November, and conversation between himself and Washington led to a small scientific experiment. Local people insisted that the creek at the bottom of the hill could be set on fire, and Paine and Washington decided to test the story. Embarking in a scow, they took up positions at opposite ends, each armed with a lighted roll of cartridge paper. Meanwhile soldiers, stationed on the bank for the purpose, began to disturb the mud in the bottom of the river with long poles. Bubbles arose, and fire "took" from Washington's light, descending thence to the surface of the water. The amateur scientists were duly convinced that an "inflammable air," in other words a marsh gas, arose from the mud.

The visit was a social success, but it failed in its purpose of influencing Congress. A movement was growing to let the states distribute rewards, and presently New York State led the way. By spring of 1784, Paine was offered his choice of two New York farms; in June he was officially granted the estate of a Tory at New Rochelle which he thought must be worth at least a thousand guineas.

Here was compensation at last! To celebrate taking possession, Paine gave a village fete. In the highest spirits, he had a word for everyone and could be seen sitting in the shade to help preparations, "cutting or breaking sugar to be used in some agreeable liquids." But he only talked of living there; for the moment he needed to remain in Bordentown.

Washington, persevering in kindly intentions, now wrote to Madison, Richard Henry Lee, and various other members of the Virginia Assembly on Paine's behalf. Thomas Jefferson, whose political opinions were in many ways similar to Paine's, also pressed his merits on Madison. A bill was introduced in the Virginia Assembly to grant him land worth four thousand pounds. It very nearly passed, and would have done so had not Paine's article on the Virginian land claims offended so many.

Undaunted, Washington recommended Paine to the State of Pennsylvania, which, though tardily, prepared to follow the example of New York. If any state were to reward Paine, it must most properly have been Pennsylvania. At this time, however, the state was split by another controversy in which Paine strongly opposed the radical party.

The Bank of North America, which had been started by Paine's original impulse, had been chartered by the state as well as Congress. By the end of the war, shortage of coin had led to agitation for paper money in which the farmers and small businessmen could pay their debts. The bank, whose stockholders would be damaged by inflation, threw its influence on the opposite side. The radicals thereupon called for a petition to repeal the bank charter.

Paine's connection with the bank was close; and besides, it was his opinion that a contract with the state was not like a law which could be repealed in response to political change. While subject to review once in a generation, a contract ought by its very nature to involve some permanency. In fact, the movement to repeal the bank charter was interfering with rights which were essential to the people. It was attacking the principle upon which all business which individuals did with the state must needs be founded.

This view of Paine's led him in typical fashion to side against his influential supporters. The radical position was that tight money worked hardship on the poor. No sooner was Paine seen to be taking the side of the rich than he was accused in the public press of letting his pen out for hire, of being a drunkard, of having already received too great a reward for what he had done, and of having no scruples against using his talents for the ruin of his country. Meanwhile, he was unable to press his merits on Timothy Matlack and other friends in the Assembly, lest it be imagined that he was using the affair to levy blackmail and seeking to be bought off.

In these circumstances, Paine was possibly lucky to get anything at all from Pennsylvania. The committee appointed to consider his case recommended five hundred pounds as a temporary recompense while the subject was being discussed. This the Assembly duly paid as the price for shelving the issue. His acceptance did not deter Paine from defending the bank and exposing the fallacies of paper money.

Not yet despairing of Congress, Paine put in a claim for six thousand dollars as reimbursement for his expenses in the nation's service and arrears of his salary as secretary to the Committee for Foreign Affairs. Part of this last was genuinely owing, but Congress preferred not to hash over the Deane affair or to recall the censure on Paine for indiscretion. In consequence, Paine was granted a "gratification" of three thousand dollars in return for his services.

These various grants served to provide Paine with a small income, as well as an estate which could be farmed. It is true that he had no aptitude for farming, but his personal wants were modest. For the moment at least, he was freed from monetary cares and, gladly throwing off the burden of writing history, decided to devote his life to science.

Paine's interest in experiment was great, and his bent was practical. At a time, however, when a man must not only devise but construct apparatus, he was unskilled with his hands. His training as a corsetmaker does not seem to have helped him in this respect. He did not, moreover, possess that eye for design which led Franklin to create an efficient stove or Benjamin Thompson, the Tory, later Count Rumford, to put a hole in the handles of saucepans so that they could be hung up. Paine did the best he could for himself by hiring John Hall, a carpenter with mechanical skills who had just emigrated from England.

Paine worked with Hall for about two years; and they got on well together, except that Hall did more practical work than Paine and noticed his employer was not remarkable for rising early and getting down to the job. At the end of 1786, Paine sent over to Franklin a "smokeless candle" with a hole down the length of it which was supposed to draw smoke to the base and prevent its obscuring the flame. Franklin was willing to try out this curious product; and the two dined together on New Year's Day for the purpose. After tea they solemnly blew a gentle current through their candles and decided together that it improved the light.

In the following spring, an interesting man appeared in Bordentown. This was John Fitch, who, though without mechanical training or access to the best steam engines from England, had devoted himself to the task of making a steamboat. There were no shortcuts for Fitch. He had to work out the proportions of his own boilers and condensers, and design his own paddles, stumbling through errors which other people had already made and avoided. Without resources himself, he had to raise funds for construction of vast apparatus which, it stood to reason, was expensive.

Nothing daunted Fitch. He had with him at the time he came to Bordentown a little model. Paine, who had discussed the subject of steamboats with William Henry eight years before, who had a mechanic working for him, and who was possessed of cash, looked to Fitch like an ideal partner. Paine, unwilling to risk his newfound independence by investing in such a dubious concern, missed his chance to go down in history as an inventor. Fitch wandered off with his obsession, heading for failure, for success, for failure again, for despair and suicide. All these Paine might have been forced to share with him, had he invested in the project. John Hall, who was also interested in the subject at this time, did some work on steamboats later; but he was lucky enough not to have any money.

Meanwhile, Paine had thrown aside the smokeless candle, which cannot have deluded Franklin for long, and turned in another direction. Watching idly the great blocks of ice rolled down by the Schuylkill River in spring and reflecting on the difficulties of bridging where piers were subjected to such perils, he soon conceived the idea of a single-span arch.

It is interesting to find that, though Paine never admitted the fact, it is highly likely that the idea of this bridge was not his own. In 1779, a French architect had constructed a model of a single-span bridge and had placed it on exhibition the following winter. If Paine on his trip to France in 1781 had not seen this, he certainly could have read an account of it which was published in 1783. Like his political opinions, Paine's scientific ideas were not entirely original. He was used to picking them up and making them his own, without quite knowing where they had come from. At all events, the two designs were similar. Both were iron bridges supported by a single arch, constructed with a number of interlocking ribs; both could be assembled and disassembled at will. It is probable, however, that Paine had only casual memories of his predecessor's work to guide him. At all events, he says he took inspiration from the construction of a spider's web and that in commemoration of the United States he decided to construct his arch with thirteen ribs.

However it was inspired, Paine found that to work out the details of a single-arch bridge was by no means easy. Indeed, at first he had thought of a bridge of a number of arches; and only when he discovered that a petition was before the Assembly to construct a three-arch bridge across the Schuylkill did he finally produce a wrought-iron model of a single arch which he demonstrated to Franklin and Rittenhouse in December, 1787, by getting three men to stand on it.

On New Year's Day it was exhibited at the State House. Paine had hoped to interest Robert Morris in it, but the financier had too many irons in the fire. Next he suggested that the Assembly charter a subscription company to raise $33,330, which he estimated to be the cost of construction. The matter was talked about, but the Assembly did not proceed as far as taking action. Paine, whose "temporary" compensation of five hundred pounds had also led to nothing, lost patience with the Assembly. His resources were not inexhaustible; he had been paying a mechanic for two years and had constructed several large model bridges in wood or iron. It was time he got some compensation for his labors.

Franklin, who had long ago forgotten the bitterness of the Deane affair, was hopeful about chances of raising money for the bridge in France. His own inventions and discoveries had been welcomed there; and he had found the Academy of Sciences in Paris far more enterprising than the American Philosophical Society, which owed the greater part of its reputation to himself. His connections, both political and social, were at Paine's disposal. Indeed Franklin, whose own family had been a disappointment, regarded Paine as his political and scientific offspring.

The prospect of a change was grateful to Paine, who had by now stuck to a single career for two solid years. Fate, which seemed unable to start a revolution without him, directed his choice. It was 1787. As unprepared for the French Revolution as he had once been for the American, Paine embarked with his model bridge to seek a fortune in France.

1787-91
A New Age in Europe

When Paine arrived in France in the early summer of 1787, the old regime had two more years to run. Except occasionally, it had no idea that its time was short. To be sure, the king was weak, the queen unpopular, the finances of the state in parlous condition. The middle class was greedy for power; the aristocracy and church were corrupt; the intellectuals were tearing down faith and spreading strange doctrines; unemployment was rife in the big towns, especially in Paris. For twenty years the situation in France had looked very much the same; but since nothing had exploded, few people saw there was immediate danger.

Thomas Jefferson, minister to France, moved in liberal circles, as did Lafayette and Franklin's friends. It was easy for Paine to listen to complaints of the regime; but France had been America's friend, and King Louis was as popular there as George III was hated. If somebody must be blamed for affairs in France, let it be the aristocracy for driving a wedge between a good king and his people.

Paine joined in talk of this kind, but his business in France concerned his bridge. He presented his model to the Academy of Arts and Sciences, which after deliberation endorsed it. Through the influence of his friends,

Paine rather hoped to get it erected over the Seine, though he was disquieted to hear that Caron de Beaumarchais had started a rival scheme which made it possible that he would lose the fruits of his labor.

The machinery of the French administration moved slowly, giving time for Paine to pay several visits to England while the business of his bridge hung fire. His father, now seventy-nine, had been ailing for some time and died before he could see his son again. Paine spent three weeks with his mother, however, though his relationship with her had always been cool. He settled on her a pension of nine shillings a week, which seems to have satisfied her modest wants. Frances Pain was now ninety and lived some years longer; but we do not know whether her son visited her.

Most of his contacts in England were on a higher level, since he could not resist the chance to meddle in politics. He was intimate in Paris with Thomas Jefferson, the American minister, who was bound to concern himself with British policy. At the moment, it looked as though the British were drifting back into a war with France.

Aware that the reputation of "Common Sense" had not been forgotten in England and Ireland, Paine thought he might have influence on the British people at large. Accordingly, he sought an interview with the secretary of M. de Brienne, Archbishop of Toulouse, who was at the moment Louis XVI's chief minister. British enmity to France, he pointed out, was an out-of-date survival nourished by popular prejudice. The time had come to make a change, especially as British temper had been sobered by defeat in the last war. A timely pamphlet on the advantages of peace to both countries might have a great effect, provided that the French ministry had not decided privately on a rupture.

Reassured on this point, Paine produced a political treatise attacking the policies of William Pitt, now British Prime Minister, and outlining the economic advantages of peace to both countries. Economic theory in Paine's day was not wholly understood, and his glowing accounts of French prosperity look strange in retrospect. But his criticisms of Pitt recommended him to the Parliamentary figure who was understood to be the brains of the opposition.

Edmund Burke (1729-97) was a living proof to his generation that the vitality of the British political system was not dead. He was not the sort of man who wins elections and most probably would have made no public career under democracy. He owed his seat in Parliament to a patron whose secretary he had been and who, controlling many boroughs, put in Burke to support his interests. Even when he had reached Parliament, it seemed unlikely that Burke would impress the local squires or the great magnates who composed and controlled that body.

Burke was an Irishman, for one thing, a Protestant, but a nobody and social upstart. To make matters worse, he lived with a brother and cousin who were far more Irish in manner than he, besides being untrustworthy and ambitious. His very appearance was unimpressive, with narrow frame, peering head, vast beak of a nose, and spectacles. Even his oratory, magnificently though it reads, was spoiled for his audience by his trace of a brogue, his overemotional delivery, and sheer length.

By the time that Paine met Burke through an introductory letter from Henry Laurens, no drawbacks of man-

ner, or appearance, or even of association could conceal
the fact that he was a great statesman. His unflagging industry, his extraordinary power of marshaling facts, and
the brilliance of his mind had impressed his fellows in
spite of themselves. Burke, moreover, was a statesman
of a judicious sort, one who set his face against abuses
and saw political life in terms of growth. He believed as
genuinely as Paine in freedom from aggression; he was
as ready to take up the case of the underdog; but he had
not the revolutionary conviction that things can be done
in a hurry. Thus, though unfitted in every personal way
to be the leader of the liberals of his age, Burke manifestly
had become their source of strength and embodied their
conscience.

Nothing had done more to build Burke's reputation
than his defense of the American colonies. Early in the
sixties he had seen with regret that reactionary conserva-
tism was determined to put the colonies back in their
proper place. He foresaw the struggle that must ensue and
understood its importance. In typical fashion, he proceeded to make himself master of the problem, acting for
several years as agent for the New York Assembly, and
seizing every opportunity of discussing colonial affairs
with those who knew them at first hand.

It was clear to Burke that an enormous explosion of
energy had taken place in the American colonies during
his lifetime. Shipping, fisheries, wealth, and trade had
grown and were still growing at a fantastic rate. The colo-
nials were striking out for themselves, building new institutions, founded on English principles, but freely adapted
to their different way of life. This energy, this manifesta-
tion of freedom, could not be repressed or dammed up. It

was useless for Parliament to insist on the letter of ancient rights. The true statesman must work out a partnership which suited the new forces that were at work.

In agreement with this view, Burke had spoken out against the Stamp Act and in general against all the oppressive measures of the British right up to the outbreak of war. This, too, he had opposed, thinking it far better that England should give the Americans a present of liberty than fight them about it.

Since this had been Burke's constant position, it was natural for Paine to suppose they were on the same side. In truth, however, as it must have been clear to Burke from the start, their opinions were different. Burke never had believed in American independence. To him an institution such as the British Empire, called into existence to solve complex problems of the past, was not be to tossed over simply because it had grown outdated. It might need to be changed, enlarged, regenerated; but its roots in tradition, its virtues (and every human institution has some), its contribution to stability must be preserved. He deplored the break between England and America because both lost by it. Yet if political separation became inevitable, he wanted the old ties of language, common law, trade, and religion to be binding. The evils wrought to both sides by a war were worse than independence.

This is a far cry from "Common Sense" who, after fifteen months in America, saw separation as obvious, easy, and desirable. Paine looked on 1776 as the seed-time of a glorious future. Burke regarded it as the wrenching of a limb from the parent tree to the hurt of both. Paine thought of the new American republic as an example to the world which should usher in a happier age. Burke wished America well, but shook his head sadly and even in a prophetic moment foresaw in the distance the Civil War.

These differences between the two men were obscured for the moment because Burke was interested in Paine, who was dazzled by a richer and more subtle mind than he was used to. Paine was revisiting a country in which he had always been an outsider and obscure. Without any gradual climb which might have prepared him, he was immediately received into political circles. Not unnaturally he did not know where he himself stood on important issues, simply because they looked quite different from this viewpoint. Even those who had agreed with him in America had changed in Europe. France needed reform, but Lafayette was a royalist there. Burke, too, was a royalist, even though George III at this time was mad. Burke and his party were hoping that the Prince of Wales, being appointed regent, would bring them into power.

An alliance between Paine and Burke was largely cemented by their distrust of Pitt, the Prime Minister. Pitt, as it happened, was an idealist too and dreamed of reform. The difference between his private views and Burke's was often not great; but he was a king's man, chief supporter not just of monarchy, but precisely of George III, who symbolized in person everything that Paine had learned to hate about England.

Paine's acquaintance with Burke ripened fast. He paid a visit to him and then took a tour with him around the iron factories of the Midlands. The prospects for his bridge were not advancing in France, and he decided to try it out in England. He took out patents, submitted his designs to British experts, and discussed them with the Walker brothers of Sheffield, proprietors of the largest iron foundry in the country. At the end of that summer of 1788, he agreed with the Walkers that they should construct an experimental span at their works in Rotherham, where he would supervise the project. He planned an arch of two hundred and fifty feet, but discovered that it was too large to be constructed under cover, while English weather was a drawback to working out of doors. He compromised on ninety feet, which were duly completed the following spring. The bridge was erected between a wall of the furnace and a nearby brick building and successfully loaded with twice its weight in iron to test its strength.

Thus encouraged, Paine ordered a 110-foot span, which was to be shipped in pieces to London, exhibited there for a small fee, and put up for sale. Half the proceeds were to go to the Walkers and the rest to Paine, who had however borrowed from a former Philadelphia merchant, Peter Whiteside, in return for a share in his profit from the venture.

In August, 1790, the bridge was erected near Paddington, now part of London, in an open field. The operation was a considerable trouble to Paine because the foreman fell off the scaffolding on the first day and tore a great piece out of his leg. Paine was forced to take over himself and managed fairly well, though he hated the long hours and was irritated beyond endurance by people who came to view the contraption and managed to pass the gate and inspect it free.

It was up at last, and Paine congratulated himself that he had started "a pretty general revolution in Bridge Architecture." No sale took place, however; and meanwhile political matters were absorbing his interest. Paine's attention wavered. There was the money he had invested, and yet the state of the world was more important.

He had not been in France more than a month or two; he had certainly not visited England before he began to see himself as intermediary between the English Whigs and Jefferson. How fortunate that America had no minister in England! He urged Jefferson to advise against one. A minister would of necessity be dealing with Pitt and the Tories, the court party in power. The future of England lay with Burke, Fox, Portland, and the Whigs. Paine was sure of it, and indeed they were so themselves. The degeneration of the king's health, together with the close alliance between Fox and the heir apparent, made them certain as 1788 wore on that Pitt must fall. Jefferson, who agreed with Paine that the Whigs were the party of the future, was glad to keep up relations with them. It would not do for the minister to France to intrigue openly with the opposition party in London, but a go-between without official position could make the connection.

Thus it was that Jefferson wrote to Paine, who passed on information to Burke without actually stating who his correspondent was. In return Paine wrote to Jefferson about the English situation, quoting freely from the opinions of his Whig friends. The arrangement was in no sense underhand. The little trickle of confidential information was of assistance to both parties, while Paine felt himself in a position to do America political service.

This was already the state of affairs on New Year's Day of 1789, that fatal occasion when Louis XVI, having vainly attempted to stave off bankruptcy, was reduced to summoning the States General to advise him. This general assembly was a long-dead institution, unwieldy and un-

suited to the times of 1789; but the vital fact was that
Louis had called in the people of France to consult with
him about their future.

A great wave of emotion surged through France. It
might be true that most of those who felt it understood
only in the vaguest terms what they desired. French intellectuals had successfully over many years undermined
men's confidence in the church, the aristocracy, the feudal
system and in general what was soon to be called the old
regime. But in the place of these they had put nothing but
a faith in brotherhood and human nature as vague as the
Declaration of Independence, which proclaims on behalf
of slave-holding states that all men are created equal. No
practical policies, no parties, very few leaders emerged
to guide the revolution which was coming. There was
rather an immense expectation. Old men saw visions and
young men dreamed dreams. As that momentous year
stumbled on its way, the eyes of the civilized world were
fixed on France where the old was giving birth to something strange and—if men's hopes were a clue—to something wonderful. It was a moment when the spirits of
young men everywhere were lifted up. The poet Words-
worth summed up the feeling later in a famous line: "Bliss
was it in that dawn to be alive."

Enthusiasm is all very well, but for the practical business of transforming the government of France, experience was needed; while owing to nature of the old regime,
experience was wanting.

Circumstances gave unusual importance to Lafayette
and Thomas Jefferson, who had already helped to establish a union of states on democratic principles. Lafayette,
who in America had followed the leadership of Washing-

ton, was soon to prove himself unable to direct a revolution. Thomas Jefferson, who was in any case recalled by the middle of the summer, was in a delicate position, being accredited officially to the court of King Louis, who had soon fallen into the hands of the reactionaries.

In this situation, Paine was in a position to keep Burke and his friends in touch with the plans of the French moderate reformers. Jefferson gave practical advice to Lafayette, knew most of his secrets, and was at one time, though unwillingly, induced to lend his house for a private meeting at which the revolutionaries discussed plans. Paine was eager to transmit what he could to the Whigs because he too was riding the enthusiasm of the times. It seemed impossible to him that the glorious revolution in France would not spread to England, where his old experience of poverty and opposition had convinced him that a change was needed as badly as in France.

He was not alone in the feeling, but Burke and the Whigs did not share it. For a short while, circumstances had conspired to obscure the division between Paine's thought and Burke's. But now when Paine suggested that the Whigs should promote revolution under guise of reform, Burke answered in anger: "Do you mean to propose that I, who have all my life fought for the British constitution, should devote the wretched remains of my days to conspire its destruction?"

Paine must have known from this time that a great gulf existed between himself and the English Whigs, but they still remained the party with whom he had to deal. There was no personal quarrel between himself and Burke, and the logic of events might change the picture. Meanwhile, in the fall of 1789, he went to Paris to see the revolution for himself. Thomas Jefferson, as we have seen, had gone home; but Paine wrote to President Washington directly on the subject. There was no one but Lafayette who was in as good a position to inform the President about happenings in France.

There was a new American representative in Paris. Gouverneur Morris, who had gone over to Europe on business for Robert Morris, had been given an official mission in Paris in connection with the payments of the American debt. The withdrawal of Jefferson left him as the only American with diplomatic status and, in effect, as the minister. But Morris was a very different man from Jefferson. His friends were aristocratic, and he listened to their well-justified complaints of persecution, and actual physical danger. Morris, in other words, felt himself accredited to the old regime of France, whereas Thomas Jefferson had leaned toward the new. The difference was a question of discretion and taste, for no one at this moment could tell either what France was or what she would be.

Gouverneur Morris had always been cool toward Paine, but they knew each other and had friends in common. He visited Paine's bridge in 1790 and thought it uglier than he had been led to suppose. Paine stayed with him now in Paris, at least for a while; and the two discussed the progress of events.

At the end of 1789, Paris was still aflame with triumph over the fall of the Bastille on July 14. In actual fact, the Bastille, though symbol of tyranny and a mysterious prison into which men disappeared without trial, contained at the time of its storming only seven prisoners, and these of the commonest criminal sort. Its chief importance had been as an arsenal in which the forces of reaction had

been gathering weapons for a coup. The attack had really
shown that it was impossible to control the Paris mob,
swollen by immigrants from the countryside drawn thither
by excitement or in hope of work. There was famine in the
country because of a bad harvest, and the impatience of
the poor was already showing itself in violent acts. Châteaux were being looted, and muniment rooms with ancient documents confirming seigneurial rights were going
up in flames. Now the people had taken a direct hand in
the struggle which was going on about reforms in Paris.

Lafayette and the constitutional monarchists were for
the moment confirmed in power by the fall of the Bastille.
The king had given way; the forces of reaction had been
shattered; and decent men had rallied behind Lafayette,
forming a national guard to put down disorder. It was
politic to flatter the mob by proclaiming the fall of the Bastille as a glorious occasion. If Lafayette and his friends had
any conception of how many such occasions were to
follow now that the mob had tasted blood, they were pru-
dently not looking ahead. Lafayette presented the key of
the Bastille to Paine so that it might be forwarded direct
to Washington as an official gift from one free nation to
another. Paine accepted it in the spirit in which it was
meant. Already he found himself spiritually at home in
revolutionary France. Opinions which he had long personally held, but which had seemed unsuitable in the puz-
zling climate of the old Paris, came back to him with new
force. Lafayette did not go far enough. Away with monarchy! His ideas were focusing upon a republic.

It was on this trip to France that Paine became intimate
with the French philosopher and republican Condorcet.
They knew and admired each other's works, while Con-

dorcet was the center of a group of like-minded persons who were attempting to carry revolution far beyond anything dreamed of by Lafayette. They were windy, inexperienced politicians, full of noble theories but not above intrigue in practice. At the moment they formed what appeared a left wing in opposition to the constitutional monarchists, and they were becoming known as the party of the Gironde.

In the general confusion of French affairs, political parties were still undefined, so that it was possible for Paine to be drawn into Girondist circles while keeping the trust of Lafayette. Paine was beginning by now to draft another pamphlet on basic principles, and Lafayette could write to Washington about it: " 'Common Sense' is writing for you a brochure in which you will see a portion of my adventures. The result will be I hope happy for my country and for humanity."

By the spring of 1790, Paine was back again in England superintending the erection of his bridge in Paddington. His French visit had deepened and strengthened the radical opinions which were natural to his mind. By this time it was clear to him that he had less in common with the Whigs than he did with certain radical groups who were not represented in the British Parliament.

1791

The Rights of Man

While this change was going on in Paine's thought, Burke also was making up his mind about the revolution. There is no doubt that he and Paine saw essentially the same thing. The spirit of violent revolution, the desire to scrap the past and start again, the temperament which sees everything in black or white is so familiar to us after Marx, after Lenin, after Mao that it is not easy to put ourselves back in the days when it was novel. What made it harder to recognize in 1789 was the confusion and lack of leadership in France. This was no emergence of a long-established underground group, but a new and terrible spirit rolling over men like a flood. To Paine, the optimist, it was the spirit of the American Revolution. As a newcomer there he had never understood how completely the United States grew from its own past. To Burke, the admirer of the slowly developing British constitution, what he saw was simply the spirit of destruction.

It is hard to say what first alarmed Burke, but it may easily have been some information passed on to him by Paine. At all events, he turned to the task of understanding France those remarkable powers which he had already displayed in studying the American colonies. He sought for knowledge everywhere and was as eager to talk to aristocrats fleeing from terror as to talk to Paine.

Everything that Burke heard about the revolution dis-
turbed him. The Assembly with eager enthusiasm was
sweeping away the old institutions of church and state.
Property rights were being transferred from one class to another, often by violence. Great châteaux or ancient charters
were burning while their owners fled for their lives. The
lands of the Church had been arbitrarily confiscated for the
nation. The King and Queen, escorted to Paris by a rude
and terrifying mob, were prisoners in all but name. Meanwhile the Assembly, instead of hastening to provide the
new regime with a workable constitution, dawdled away
its time on windy declarations about the rights of man.

Something terrible had been unleashed which, under
pretext of setting men free, would bring uncounted miseries on the people of Europe. The principles of Burke's
political life warned him that wholesale destruction of the
restraints of the past would lead to unheard-of excesses.
In 1789-90, while Paine was renewing his ardor in France,
Burke had made up his mind. It was time to warn his
countrymen against the French Revolution.

Burke opened his campaign with a violent attack in
Parliament early in 1790, which he followed up by adver-
tising a "public letter" in which he would shortly justify
his position. Actually *Reflections on the French Revolution* did not appear until November, for the very richness
of Burke's mind imposed delay. It is a work of burning
sincerity and matchless rhetoric written by a man of genius. It is not, as Paine was to imply, merely a moving plea
for the romantic past. Nor is it only, as conservatives
boasted, a brilliant prophecy of events to come: the massacres, the year of the Terror, the corruption and cynicism

which followed, the dictatorship, and the long tragedy of the Napoleonic Wars. It is indeed these things, but it is much more. Into the *Reflections* Burke poured the convictions of his political life. Hear him for instance, on the question of whether to reform or abolish outworn institutions: "They have cast their roots wide and deep, and . . . by long habit, things more valuable than themselves are so adapted to them, and in a manner interwoven with them, that the one cannot be destroyed without notably impairing the other."

The National Assembly had swept away the past in France and was trying to legislate a brave new world without foundations. Public standards of taste and morality had gone with the rest, with the result that every excess was possible. In the end, nothing would be final in France but sheer force; and the Assembly was already degenerating into cliques, each plotting the destruction of the others.

Burke had a profound sense of the complicated network of influences which has made us what we are. This rendered him contemptuous of the simplicities of the new thought. It was not true, he cried, that human nature is naturally good and needs only to be freed from the chains of custom and convention. It was not true either that the General Will, a mysterious object which might as well be embodied in a dictator as in a popular vote, is right by instinct. Burke resisted the idea of the totalitarian state, which is that men must be reduced to the same level so that even local and family connections cannot interpose between them and the government. "We have not been drawn or trussed," he writes indignantly, "in order that we may be filled, like stuffed birds in a museum, with chaff and rags, and paltry, blurred shreds of paper about the rights of man." It is a graphic dismissal of what we have come to know as propaganda.

The impact of the *Reflections* on British opinion was enormous. It put an end to that hopeful optimism with which idealists had greeted the new dawn. But the most shattering of its practical effects was the splitting of the Whig party. It had been natural for Fox and other Whig politicians to share the idealism of Jefferson or Paine. It had even been good political tactics in their game of opposition to Pitt, who was only willing to let the French manage their own affairs provided that England was not stirred by their example. Through the action of Burke, the Whigs were so divided that they could not agree on a common policy. Thus Pitt's increasing alarm at the spread of radical ideas in England led almost without opposition to repressive measures.

While Burke was composing his momentous speech to Parliament, Paine too, as Lafayette had written to Washington, was marshaling his thoughts. But when he heard that Burke would shortly publish a "public letter," he decided to wait until it was out and to draft his own pamphlet in the form of an answer. This in itself gave opportunities to his vigorous, argumentative style. In addition, he understood that Burke's reputation for liberal thought made his present position doubly important. His matchless eloquence, brilliant mind, and wide information must produce a powerful effect. He had to be answered immediately and with force. So strongly did Paine see the necessity of this that he restrained his own impatience though the promised letter was constantly delayed, and rumor was busy saying that Burke was unable to finish it.

His relationship with Burke was still personally friendly enough for them to meet several times, though they kept off the subject of France. Since Fox and others of the Whigs still supported the revolution, there was no reason for Paine's connection with them to be broken off entirely. Indeed, the contrary was the case. Paine's self-elected position as unofficial American diplomat was precious to him. He picked up what information he could, reproached Lafayette, around whom troubles were gathering thick and fast, for being a careless correspondent, and dashed off letters to Jefferson and Washington with news.

He was making his way at the same time in other British circles, less aristocratic but certainly more to his mind. English intellectuals had not as a whole taken up the French Revolution; but there was a radical group around the philosopher William Godwin in London, and other groups in the provinces, containing, for instance, the scientist Priestley, who discovered oxygen. Such people were kept in touch with one another by the formation of radical societies, some old, some new, but all affected by the efficient organizational techniques of the French Jacobins.

Most venerable among these was the Revolution Society, originally founded to commemorate the British revolution of 1688 by having a dinner to drink to the downfall of King James on the anniversary of that event. In the 1770s, after Wilkes and Horne Tooke had shown the way, the Revolution Society developed into a radical organization with a secret inner group and corresponding branches throughout the country.

Other clubs soon followed the example of the Revolution Society. The Society for Constitutional Information, established in 1780 to press for moderate constitutional reform, took a more radical turn. In 1792 to the scandal of society, the London Corresponding Society was founded by a shoemaker and was composed almost entirely of the working class. Loud discussions of the principles of the French Revolution or formal greetings sent across the Channel were intermingled with demands for the remodeling of the English church and state. To such societies, Paine was a natural champion; and they prepared to spread his forthcoming pamphlet throughout the nation.

Paine's *Rights of Man,* his reply to Burke, was published in two parts, the first dedicated to Washington and appearing on his birthday in 1791; and the second, dedicated to Lafayette, about a year later. Though in form an answer to Burke, the *Rights* is far more than this. It is a vindication of the French and American revolutions, an indictment of the British system, a statement of principles, and an outline of plans. It is in fact a tremendous book, a blueprint of revolution, abounding in practical advice, rose-colored ideals, trenchant criticism, sweeping generalization, profound at one moment and superficial at the next. If it lacks the eloquence of Burke, it is great in irony, in mastery of a vivid phrase. It speaks plainly to plain people, never asking complexity of thought or profound knowledge or balancing of interests, one against another. "Men have only to think," cries Paine, "and they will neither act wrong nor be misled." It is a saying for the multitude, not the aristocrat. The age of the common man had found a prophet.

In Paine's actual controversy with Burke, it is not easy to decide which of them comes off victor. Burke's ability to understand the complexities of human history is far greater than Paine's. Paine never puts himself into the past or sees what has happened from the point of view of its own day. To him, all history which does not agree with the understanding of an eighteenth-century rationalist is folly. His judgments of the past are sweeping and unsound, while his hopes for the future are never sobered by the lessons of history. Thus a striking contrast between the two is the way in which Burke can prophesy the events of the next thirty years, the excesses of the revolution to come and the war which will sweep over Europe. Meanwhile Paine, looking around complacently, hardly two years before the Reign of Terror, exclaims: "Who has the National Assembly brought to the scaffold? None."

On the other hand, because Burke was committed to defending the past as a necessary part of the future, he overlooked the fact that institutions, like buildings, sometimes do collapse completely. In fact he laid himself open to the criticism that he was romantically defending the old regime without considering how many people had suffered under it. In a famous purple passage, Burke contrasted Marie Antoinette at the height of her beauty with the virtual prisoner that she was now. Chivalry, one of the civilizing influences of the past, is dead when a woman, a queen, can be so treated. Burke's point is well taken, yet an even better one is contained in Paine's reply that his adversary "pities the plumage and forgets the dying bird."

So different are Burke and Paine that the merits of their writings cannot be summed up by how they attack each other. *The Rights of Man* had an impact because it had something to say of a positive nature. In essence, it was not original; but Paine knew how to apply theories to the situations of his time.

The rights of man, says Paine, are of two sorts. The first

are natural rights which we were all born with, such as the right to hold our own opinions, and the right to seek happiness without injuring others. Civil rights, on the other hand, are natural rights which have been surrendered to the group as the price of community living. The right to decide our own disputes, for instance, is impractical in daily life and must be given up in return for a fair trial. The task of government is to enforce our civil rights; and its authority rests on the consent which we gave (and give) by living together.

This theory of government is not based on actual history but on the assumption that individuals first came together voluntarily and on equal terms. How governments resting on force, or on wealth, or on the wisdom of a small group arose, the theory does not say. It merely condemns them on the ground that men have lost in them an equality they once possessed. It ignores the fact that human happiness can be attained in a variety of ways. In fact, its appeal is less to the political scientist than to the human conscience, which tells us plainly there is something in it.

This simple view, because it concerns itself with fundamentals, can be used to criticize complex institutions which, as Burke pointed out, have gradually developed in response to practical problems and which, like human nature, are partly good and partly bad. These are particularly easy to condemn if their weaknesses are attributed not to the individuals who made them, but to the institutions themselves, which have perverted the natural goodness of mankind. To be sure, there is a flaw in Paine's reasoning here; but once again, there is something in it. Institutions do often in fact pervert individuals, and simplifications can sometimes be applied to tangled problems with fruitful effect.

The result of all this is that although we have to discount a great deal that Paine says, either because his economics were unsound or his optimism not justified in view of later events, again and again he strikes a note which is profoundly right.

"Government is not a trade which any man or body of men has a right to set up and exercise for his own emolument, but is altogether a trust."

"When in countries that are called civilized, we see age going to the work-house, and youth to the gallows, something must be wrong in the system of government."

As usual, moreover, Paine has a splendid ability to drive a point home in vivid language.

"It is related that in the canton of Berne, in Switzerland, it had been customary from time immemorial, to keep a bear at the public expense, and the people had been taught to believe, that if they had not a bear, they should all be undone. It happened some years ago, that the bear, then in being, was taken sick, and died too suddenly to have his place immediately supplied with another.

"During the interregnum the people discovered, that the corn grew and the vintage flourished, and the sun and moon continued to rise and set, and every thing went on the same as before, and, taking courage from these circumstances, they resolved not to keep any more bears; 'for,' said they, 'a bear is a very voracious, expensive animal, and we were obliged to pull out his claws, lest he should hurt the citizens.'

"The story of the bear of Berne was related in some of

the French newspapers, at the time of the flight of Louis XVI, and the application of it to monarchy could not be mistaken in France; but it seems that the aristocracy of Berne applied it to themselves, and have since prohibited the reading of French newspapers."

It is easy to list anecdotes or pronouncements of this kind which are as pertinent today as they were then, the easier perhaps because the nineteenth and twentieth centuries have been an age of revolution. We are used to tearing down in order to build up, to simplifying complexities into slogans. Essentially, Paine is a modern man, whereas Burke understands the long developments of history. If some of Paine appears out of date today, enough remains to explain the extraordinary impact of *The Rights of Man* when it was published. *Common Sense* was all past history now. Here was the dawn of a new age, and Paine was its prophet.

The first edition of *The Rights of Man* consisted only of a few copies, since the authorities put pressure on the publisher to abandon the issue. But a work of this kind is not easily suppressed. The sheets already printed were taken over by another publisher and issued less than two months after the original date. By this time, Paine was already in France preparing an edition there. It goes without saying that his impact on America was tremendous. John Adams' *Discourses on Davila,* which had just come out with a violent attack on the French Revolution, were literally snowed under by a vast number of letters and tracts supporting Paine. Almost single-handed he had changed American opinion, which had been swinging with Adams against the Revolution. Meanwhile, in England the radical clubs had reprinted twenty-five thousand copies to be sold for a nominal sum or given away throughout England and Ireland.

The sweeping success of *The Rights of Man,* fantastic for its day, alarmed the government of England. William Pitt, who had become Prime Minister after the American war when he was still only twenty-four years old, had so guided England's recovery from that disaster that she was now more prosperous than ever. Nor had Pitt set his face against needed reforms. His approach to them was the cautious one of a practical statesman; but he laid plans for enlarging the franchise, abolishing the slave trade, and establishing national insurance, family allowances, and many other useful things which can be organized in peacetime by a man who sets his mind on them. Pitt's tragedy was that he had no talent and no taste for war, yet war inevitably was to be forced upon him.

He would not recognize this yet, sticking blindly to the position that the revolution was a French affair, no business of England's. Yet when societies, modeled on the Jacobins and encouraged by French enthusiasm, appeared in England, Pitt could hardly ignore the dangers which menaced him. He knew reforms were needed which at the present pace would take a generation. He even knew that England, already humming with the industrial revolution, was producing new social problems faster than solutions. He could see from the example of France that it was fatal to throw the door wide open to the forces of progress, letting every sort of thing come in. Thus his wisest course for the moment seemed to him one of drawing back from any reforms while exerting pressure to keep the lid on a boiling pot. If only the French Revolution would let him alone! Burke saw that it would not; but

Pitt, interrupted in reforms on which his heart was set, could not bear to.

Pitt's attitude soon produced repressive measures in England. We have already seen that influence was exerted to keep the *Rights* from coming out at all. Presently, with at least semi-official encouragement, there were loyal demonstrations, some of which got out of hand. On July 14, 1791, for instance, a series of radical dinners was organized in a number of towns to celebrate the anniversary of the taking of the Bastille. Inflammatory speeches were made and feeling rose high. In Birmingham, radical leaflets were scattered in the street and a church was chalked "This barn to let." In answer, the loyal mob rose, wrecked dissenting meeting-houses, and burned the house and library of the great scientist Priestley. In fact, the tumult went on for four days until dragoons had to be brought in to restore order among crowds still chanting their war cries of "No Philosophers!" or "Church and King!"

Demonstrations such as these, some of them actually started by local magnates who gave rustics a guinea to burn Tom Paine in effigy, were countered by the radicals with increasing noise. New branches of the societies were founded; more meetings were held, speeches made, letters written. In November, the Revolution Society's annual dinner in London was attended by a select group of two hundred and fifty with one of the Walkers, bridge builders for Paine, in the chair. One of the toasts was: "Mr. Paine with thanks for his Defense of the Rights of Man." This in itself was harmless enough, but Paine's answering toast was "To the Revolution of the World."

The second part of *The Rights of Man* was not yet out on this occasion, though it was due shortly. Meanwhile

Paine, riding the crest of a great wave, had already done something almost more alarming to Pitt's government than his publications in England.

As we have seen, Paine had gone to France to oversee the French edition of the first part of his *Rights*. He was still there on the twentieth of June when the King in desperation escaped from Paris to join the royalist garrison in Metz. Caught and returned, the King had lost such authority as the new constitution had left him. During his absence, Paris was in a turmoil. Indeed Paine, who had been out to see what was doing in the streets and most especially at the palace, was caught without his revolutionary tricolor cockade, mistaken for an aristocrat, and nearly lynched.

He was not content to remain an onlooker in a time of such excitement. The Assembly wanted the King back as the figurehead which confirmed their own authority. The man in the street, outraged by the King's treachery, talked a very different language. It was time for "Common Sense" to rise again and show the way. Uncommitted to any French faction, Paine decided to put his immense reputation behind a demand for a republic. Accordingly, he composed a fiery manifesto, had it translated by a young radical friend, and plastered it across the walls of Paris. It created a tremendous sensation of precisely the kind that Paine had intended. The Assembly denounced it, but at least the subject was now in the open. Paine was the hero of a certain set, and Gouverneur Morris, whose sympathies were completely on the other side, described him resentfully as "inflated to the Eyes and big with a Litter of Revolution."

It was only natural that this republicanism should look

almost worse to Pitt than the first part of *The Rights of Man,* which, though revolutionary in tone and content, had devoted a great deal of its space to attempting to show that the French Revolution was orderly and legal. The second part of the *Rights,* which now followed, concentrated less on the French than on the British.

We need not follow Paine in his denunciation of Burke for admiring the historical development of the British constitution. We need only examine his attitude towards its present condition to see why Pitt found *The Rights of Man* subversive. Of monarchy, for instance, Paine said: "That monarchy is all a bubble, a mere court artifice to procure money, is evident (at least to me) in every character in which it can be viewed." This is a comment which might not matter in a situation where the value of monarchy is not being heatedly discussed. But with France in its present state, such words were inflammatory. Nor are they made any better by Paine's remark elsewhere: "I do not believe that monarchy and aristocracy will continue seven years longer in any of the enlightened countries of Europe."

The change that Paine calls for is a formal constitution, on the American model to be sure, but reached by the process which was then going on in France. The Houses of Parliament, representing an infinitesimal part of the country, are so involved, he points out, in the network of corporations and private establishments which have grown up through centuries that corruption is the rule rather than the exception. A convention is necessary for reform.

What is the function of government? It is to promote the general happiness. It is easy to see that the present government of England does not do so. "Why is it that scarcely any are executed but the poor?" Paine inquires; and he gives the answer that the poor are bred without morals and cast upon the world without prospects. In other words, they have no outlet but crime under the present regime.

An honest and a decent government should not be in Paine's view at all expensive. It ought easily to afford social benefits, especially since prisons, hospitals, poorhouses, and other methods of repairing social neglect cost a great deal of money. Paine proposes an inheritance tax which will sweep away the advantages of being born into the right family. The money provided may be spent on family relief; free education; birth, marriage, and funeral bonuses; employment for the poor, and similar benefits. He spends a good deal of time on calculations to prove that these are cheap to a government which has started anew on proper principles, has sworn eternal friendship with France, and has disbanded its army. The scheme is tidy and simple-sounding, and the suggestions do Paine credit. What gives them force, however, is not their practical worth, but Paine's indictment of present conditions.

"There are two classes of people to whom the laws of England are particularly hostile," he wrote, "and those the most helpless: younger children and the poor." A man who can say that to his generation will be remembered when dozens of neat plans for reform are long forgotten.

It is not surprising to find that the second part of the *Rights* was really offensive to the English authorities. Its very publication was beset by difficulties. Paine had become friendly in France with a young Scot called Thomas Christie who happened to have been sent over there on business. Through him, Paine met a printer named Thomas Chapman who undertook to bring out the second part of *The Rights of Man,* together with another edition of the first. In the middle of January, 1792, two weeks before publication day, and after printing over a hundred pages, Chapman returned the manuscript to Paine and refused to go on with the work.

Paine and Chapman disagreed on the reason for this sudden act. According to Paine, Chapman, under secret urging from the British government, had first attempted to buy the manuscript outright, which would have given him power to suppress it completely. Failing in this, he had refused to publish. Paine was convinced that he had shown the manuscript to the authorities, and he pointed out that Pitt had come forward at this precise moment with suggestions for tax reform which had been taken from his own.

However this may be, Chapman himself said that Paine turned up drunk one evening and got into a quarrel about religion with himself and his wife. At the end he had become insulting, so that Chapman, who had been getting uneasy about the *Rights,* was glad to break with him.

This accusation, which takes its place amid the long line of stories against Paine, can neither be proved nor disproved. It was certainly convenient for Chapman to blacken Paine's character during the troubles which followed on the publication of the *Rights.* Tales about Paine's drinking were up to this date uncommon, and Chapman had to admit that his condition was unusual. All the same, at times Paine did consume a good deal of liquor; and he may have occasionally taken too much. For whatever reason, Paine quarreled with Chapman and gave the second part of the *Rights* to Jordan, who had previously brought out the first.

Even the Society for Constitutional Information, to which Paine handed over his royalties, was reluctant to lend open support to the second half of *The Rights of Man*. It was too incendiary, and they perceived that it would lead them into trouble. Its success, however, was as startling as that of the first part. It presented extreme radicals with an even more sensational platform; and they rose to the occasion, bribing the poor by drink to hear it read aloud.

Paine himself was very shortly in trouble. In April, 1792, he was arrested at the anniversary dinner of the Constitution Society for a debt of two hundred pounds. He was released on bail about an hour later; but the papers, which seldom let a day go past without abusing Paine, took full advantage of the incident.

In May, Jordan, the publisher, was served with a summons to appear in court for publishing a treasonable work. To Paine's fury, Jordan did not dispute the character of the *Rights,* but merely pleaded guilty to the indictment. This incident cleared the way for a prosecution of Paine in person, and he too was served with a summons.

Meanwhile, the government issued a proclamation against seditious writings in the hope of halting the sales of *The Rights of Man*. The actual result was vastly to increase them by making a sensation out of the book. A debate in Parliament led to a statement by Dundas, the Home Secretary, deploring the circulation of Paine's pernicious doctrines and insisting that the government intended to prosecute.

Paine answered, of course, by an open letter to Dundas

in which he claimed that it was not subversive to replace the British system of "hereditary nonsense" with the representative one of America. He followed this up by a couple of letters of protest to meetings which were held by government supporters at Epsom and his old home, Lewes. These statements naturally roused the fury of those responsible for such gatherings and made more sensational news for the papers.

Paine's trial, which had been scheduled for June, was postponed till December. Meanwhile, as it became clear that the government was determined to muzzle him, there were many rumors that he had fled to France a step ahead of the police. Actually he was living quietly in London with Thomas Rickman, his old friend from Lewes, supervising more editions of the *Rights,* playing dominoes with the Rickman children, all named after prominent republicans, including Paine. His visitors included the French and American ministers and prominent radicals, such as Horne Tooke and Priestley, or the artist George Romney (1734-1802), who about this time produced a portrait of Paine that we know through reproductions. Rickman's description of Paine, which is obviously intended to counteract stories about his careless personal habits, states that, "In his dress and person he was generally very cleanly, and wore his hair cued, with side curls, and powdered, so that he looked altogether like a gentleman of the old French school." Gouverneur Morris, who was in London then, saw Paine several times and thought him drunk with conceit, daily expecting the English revolution. For his part, Morris believed he would much more likely stand in the pillory.

This was not the view of Pitt, the Prime Minister. To

his intimates he admitted that Tom Paine was quite right
in many of his criticisms, adding despairingly, "What am
I to do? As things are, if I were to encourage Tom Paine's
opinions, we should have a bloody revolution."

Paine himself was overconfident, not surprisingly when
every post brought him letters from admirers in such
quantities that he could, he thought, have kept nine secretaries busy. But what Paine said in the heat of argument
bore little relation to his considered judgment. A Frenchman who met him in July, 1791, records scornfully that
Paine told him *The Rights of Man* "could take the place
of all the books in the world." Paine even added that "if
it were in his power to demolish all the libraries in existence, he would do it without hesitation so as to destroy
all the errors of which they were the depository—and with
The Rights of Man begin a new chain of ideas and principles." It is easy to see why he always got the "headstrong
book" at Lewes.

Paine's temperament, in fact, led casual acquaintances
to suppose that he had nothing but vanity in him. This
was far from the case. At this time his practical calculations were not unsound. Somehow or other, he must provide a spark to set the revolution off. Thus, appealing directly to the radical societies and the unorganized mass of
the working class, he drafted a public letter to the government calling for the overthrow of Parliament and the
election of a national convention by every male citizen
over twenty-one. He must assuredly have known that if
the populace did not rise to support him, a second prosecution would now follow his trial for the *Rights*. Should
he stay and make this occasion a public show? There
was no profit in offering himself as a martyr unless revo-

lution should follow. But the hopes of Paine and the fears of Pitt were based on uncertainties. Nobody living understood the nature of the proletariat being created in the new industrial towns. How could the oppressed be organized, how aroused? With the example of the Paris mob before their eyes, both thought it not unreasonable to imagine that the masses might explode in England. Yet would they do so? English conditions differed very widely from those in France.

1792-93
In Dangerous Waters

While the British government was threatening Paine with prosecution, the Revolution did not stand still in France. The new constitution, completed at last by the National Assembly, was out of date before it was put in force. It provided for a limited monarchy and a Legislative Assembly, which was to contain no members of the previous one. The result was to deprive the legislature of experienced politicians and to throw power into the hands of people outside the government. The Jacobins, with their close federation of clubs and their control of the Paris mob, became the real arbiters of France's destiny.

The Austrian Emperor Leopold, brother of Queen Marie Antoinette, had been too astute a ruler to declare war on France as long as his sister was in the power of the revolutionaries. Leopold, however, died in March, 1792, leaving his throne to Francis II, an inexperienced young man of small ability who was much influenced by exiled French aristocrats, many of whom cared less for the interests of their king than for their own. War immediately threatened.

Louis and his queen were unwilling to take sides against their closest connections, but most of the parties in France were eager to fight. The monarchists hoped that war might improve the position of the Crown, while

Paine's friends, the Girondists, thought it might afford a pretext for doing away with monarchy entirely. Besides, they expected that revolution would break out in Austrian lands and would make itself permanent in France by spreading through Europe. Only the extreme left wing was against the war, and this merely because it wanted to abolish the monarchy before involving the country in an external struggle.

Reluctantly Louis was induced to consent; and if France had been in a condition to fight, a victory might indeed have improved his position. But an invasion of Belgium, then Austrian territory, merely revealed the disgraceful state of the army, which had been encouraged to chase out its officers and refuse discipline. Its failure prepared the way for a leftist uprising, which took place in Paris on August 10. The King's guard was massacred, and the royal family was lodged in prison. Lafayette, failing to rally the army in defense of the constitution, committed political suicide by fleeing to the Austrians. This signaled the utter collapse of limited monarchy, and it was soon decided to elect a convention to draw up a republican constitution. The forces of the left, which now controlled Paris, wishing the electors to have no illusions about where power lay, staged a demonstration in the form of a bloody massacre to clear the prisons of their aristocratic prisoners. They followed it by a letter suggesting that other cities do the same.

In circumstances such as these, much of the electorate was too confused or too fearful to vote. Those, however, who had always wanted the Revolution to go further now shut their eyes to the crimes by which their power had been confirmed. There was plenty of idealism left in

France which found expression for the moment in the long and windy speeches of the party of the Gironde.

These Girondists, who had come together in 1789, were not so much politicians as political theorists. They had formed the right-wing section of the republican Jacobin clubs and had been willing, though with reservations, to cooperate with Louis under the late constitution. Since, however, they truly preferred a republic, they came forward as its champions, hoping to guide the Convention into peaceable channels. They represented as a whole the middle class, in opposition to Danton, Marat, and Robespierre, who controlled the Jacobin clubs, the revolutionary Commune of Paris, and the mob.

The position of Paine in France at this time was almost above party. It is true that the second part of *The Rights of Man* was dedicated to Lafayette and that there was considerable praise of him throughout the treatise. But Paine had been the first to call for a French republic, while *The Rights of Man* had become the bible of the revolutionary movement. Almost single-handed, his admirers claimed, he had brought England to the brink of revolution. Surely the haste of Pitt's government to prosecute Paine was a sign of its weakness. It was natural that the whole of the French left, from the Girondists to Robespierre himself respected Paine.

The enthusiastic Girondists had already sponsored a decree conferring French citizenship on Washington, Paine, Priestley, and various others whom they regarded as benefactors of the human race. Washington and Priestley made no move to take up the offer; but Paine had spent almost as much time in France as he had in England since his return from America. It was not too sur-

prising that in the current excitement he should be elected
to the Convention. There was in any case no bar to choosing foreigners, since the Revolution was determined to be
international.

Paine received the notice of his election from the district of Calais, where his name had first been introduced
as a political maneuver to reserve a place for a local politician. So great was Paine's reputation, however, that it
proved impossible to withdraw him. Enthusiasts suggested
that he might be the instrument of uniting England and
France in one glorious Revolution. This notion did not
find favor with all patriots present, but he was elected all
the same. Achille Audibert, a citizen of Calais, went over
to England personally to persuade him to accept, arriving
in early September, 1792. Hard on Audibert's heels came
notification that Paine was elected for three other depart-
ments as well.

It must have been hard for Paine to decide what to do.
On the one hand, he was offered a share in constitution-
making in the second democratic republic of the age. As
he had written earlier to Washington: "After the estab-
lishment of the American Revolution, it did not appear
to me that any object could arise great enough to engage
me a second time. I began to feel myself happy in being
quiet; but I now experience that principle is not confined
to time or place, and that the ardor of '76 is capable of
renewing itself." On the other hand, there was his trial
to come, his letter to the government, not yet published,
and the prospect of an English Revolution. It is hard to
say how truly he had come to believe in this last, but fre-
quently his thoughts were optimistic.

If he absented himself from his trial, he was sure to be

condemned. England was his native land; his bridge still stood in the field at Paddington. He might not ever see either again if he left now. On the other hand, unless England arose, Paine would be pilloried, imprisoned, rendered useless to the cause for some time to come. In addition, the success of the French Revolution was essential to an English imitation.

These considerations were reinforced by Audibert's arguments. Did not the philosopher have a duty to translate his speculations into fact? The opportunity, freely offered, to bring about the golden age in France was surely greater than the bare chance of causing revolution in England.

Thus it was that Paine was swept away by forces which he could not control. His attachment to America was strong, and his letters are full of affection and longing. He wants to know how his horse Button gets along. He misses Washington, Morris, and many familiar scenes. When the tenant of his house in Bordentown died, he forgave the widow two years' rent which was owing and invited her to stay on as his guest as long as she pleased. When a young girl whom he had been fond of got married, he wrote her a letter of good wishes full of mild regret for his own bachelor state and his distance from the people and the scenes he loved. As he yielded to Audibert, he felt excitement at the prospects which *The Rights of Man* had opened for him; but he did not embark without a pang on an adventure which was to detain him long and sever old connections.

On the twelfth of September, Paine left London for Dover accompanied by Audibert and John Frost, a liberal attorney. A dramatic story is told in a life of the poet

William Blake about Paine's escape. It seems that Paine had delivered an inflammatory address at a meeting of "The Friends of Liberty." This he repeated on the following evening to friends, of whom Blake was one. The excitable poet was convinced that arrest would follow. On Paine's rising to leave, this narrative states, "Blake laid his hand on the orator's shoulder, saying, 'You must not go home, or you are a dead man.' "

This may be true, though there seems no particular reason why Paine should not have been arrested on the evening of his speech, rather than the day after. The story goes on to relate that Paine and his friends set out for Dover by an indirect route and were pursued by officers of the law, who had previously sought him in vain at Rickman's house. The travelers were held up at Dover by customs officers, but they finally put out to sea some twenty minutes ahead of the baffled pursuers, who gnashed their teeth as they arrived upon the quay.

It is a dramatic tale, but in actual fact it seems more likely that the government officers who followed in a post chaise were merely anxious to be sure that Paine was really on his way. The party was indeed held up at Dover for over an hour. Customs officers examined all their papers, opened some letters, and took down the addresses of the rest. One of these, as it chanced, was from Washington. Paine objected to its being read, but Frost took the letter and recited some of the general remarks of the American President about "the enlightened policy of the present age." Stunned, as it is said, by the tone of these and by the signature of George Washington himself, the customs men released them.

Flattering though this version may be to Washington's reputation, it hardly seems likely that minor government officials would have released so notorious a character on the strength of a letter from the head of a foreign government, however respected. Most probably Paine was delayed until some higher authority could be consulted. By the time that the matter was settled, a crowd had collected. Dover was one of the towns where Paine had once made corsets, so that local orators could have fun with his past. There was a great deal of hissing as he went aboard, and a fellow passenger began to be afraid lest they all be pelted by pebbles from the beach. Before matters reached this point, however, the packet was towed off, it being unable to get away from the wharf for lack of wind.

In this way Paine departed from England forever. "We arrived at Calais," the other passenger narrates, "and as soon as he was known to be on the shore, the people flocked to see him, and it was talked of saluting him with the guards as he passed the Place d'Armes. It rained hard, and I left him."

He got his parade, rain or no rain. The officer of the guard embraced him and presented a tricolor cockade, while a very pretty woman asked the honor of putting it in his hat. He walked to his inn attended by men, women, and children calling, "Vive Thomas Paine!" He went on to the Town Hall, where there were more embracings and a speech, which had to be translated by M. Audibert. Paine had no gift for languages and had not so far troubled himself to learn much French. It sufficed that he laid his hand on his heart while he promised to devote his life to their service. A day or two later he set out for Paris, where his appearance made a minor sensation in the Convention. He was in high spirits at his reception everywhere, though rather tired, it is said, of all the kissing.

Enthusiasm continued to support him. He took up residence at White's Hotel, which was frequented by Englishmen and Americans alike. Here he struck up a friendship with Joel Barlow, the American poet, who had also fought in the American Revolution, been active in English radical groups, and come to take part in the revival of France. That November, Paine's admirers in White's held a Festival of the Rights of Man. This started off as a British demonstration, but was shortly broadened to include well-wishers of various nationalities, deputies from the Convention, officers of the army, and two regimental bands. Paine's health was drunk amid cheers. Lord Edward Fitzgerald and Sir Robert Smyth made certain the affair would get into the British papers by publicly renouncing their titles and toasting the abolition of "feudal distinctions."

The appearance of Lord Edward Fitzgerald on the scene had raised the possibility of starting the English revolution by rebellion in Ireland. Four thousand Irish volunteers, Fitzgerald reported, were assembling when they dared and drilling secretly in preparation for the battle of freedom. He had come over to France especially to ask Paine's help. Paine brought him to the notice of his French friends and suggested that the French government subsidize the Irish rebels by a loan of two hundred thousand pounds. He even offered to go over to Ireland himself, but Fitzgerald's backers in Dublin would have none of this. An Irish-American officer and friend of Paine's, Eleazer Oswald, was finally sent over to sound out the disposition of the people. He went to Ireland in February, 1793, and returned in June with a discouraging report. The Irish were discontented but cowed; revolution was not likely.

Meanwhile, the British government was pursuing its attack on *The Rights of Man*. Loyal demonstrations multiplied. Paine's friend, the ironmaster Walker, had his windows broken and was forced to disperse the crowd with a musket. Next day they were back again, drowning his remonstrances with: "Jacobin! Damn Tom Paine!" Rude rhymes were made up about Paine; pamphlets against him were published. Some of the incidents had a ludicrous side. A Suffolk rector, for instance, paid a number of rustics two guineas to burn Paine in effigy. "An intelligent gentleman" thereupon offered another two guineas for burning the rector in effigy, to which his audience responded joyfully, erecting their bonfire in front of the parson's door.

Such demonstrations provided fuel for the papers and pamphlets against Paine. Cut off from most of his English admirers, he was forced to wonder whether his influence was really great; and doubts oppressed him. Rousing himself, however, he sent a letter to the Attorney General, who was in charge of his prosecution, protesting that he would have stayed to contest the case, had not his duty to mankind been more important. The purpose of his trial, he complained, was not to punish himself as an individual, but to attack the right of the English people to investigate new principles of government. In closing, he warned that the people of France had already taken bloody vengeance against their oppressors and that those of England, if provoked, might do the same. If the government had ever had a doubt of the wisdom of condemning Paine, it assuredly had none left after this threatening allusion to the September massacres in Paris, when fourteen hundred had been put to death amid every sort of horror.

Horne Tooke and others of his friends had already organized a fund for Paine's defense and hired Thomas Erskine, one of the most eminent lawyers of the day, to defend him. There was little, however, that Erskine could say, though he struggled to defend free thought and free speech. The jury pronounced Paine guilty without even waiting for the prosecution to sum up its case. He was declared an outlaw and *The Rights of Man* contraband. Liberals cheered Erskine when he left court, and some of them took the horses out of his carriage and drew him home in procession. But the British people did not rise; there was no revolution. The government went on to prosecute booksellers who had handled *The Rights of Man* and printers who had issued its editions.

Over the fate of Paine's iron bridge he had no further control; but the Walkers, who had invested money in the structure, were good businessmen. The bridge was eventually erected by them across the Weare river in Sunderland, where it stood until 1929, when a more modern bridge took its place. Photographs show it as a structure of iron girders with a brick abutment on either bank. The effect is utilitarian, but straightforward, so that if it has no architectural graces, it is at least content with simplicity. Years later Paine made a move through English friends to collect the money due him for use of his patents; but it proved impossible to obtain a penny. At the present moment, he was far too busy with French affairs to give thought to his own.

He had found the leadership of the Convention divided between Girondists and Jacobins, now respectively the right and left of the republican groups. The Girondists were more numerous than their opponents, but their leadership depended on the great mass of five hundred members uncommitted so far to either side. Among these Paine preferred to be counted, for though Condorcet, philosopher of the Girondists, and Brissot, their leader, were personal friends, he wished to remain a man above party.

It is interesting to imagine Paine in the French Convention, not understanding half of what was said and having his own speeches translated into French and spoken for him while he stood by the rostrum. Luckily for him, the Convention was so wordy that it was hardly necessary to follow the meaning of speeches in detail. He kept himself informed of daily business and did not hesitate to give his opinion, just as he had always done. To the Jacobins he counted as a Girondist, while the Girondists found him only a friend, by no means always a supporter. We may wonder how soon he perceived what dangerous waters he was swimming in.

He had only joined the Convention for about three weeks when he was appointed one of a committee to draft the new constitution which was to be its business. This opened, as was now usual, with a declaration of the rights of man, said to have been drawn up by Paine. In addition, he submitted a manuscript of forty-five pages full of suggestions declaring that the new French constitution would serve as a blueprint for the revolution of the world. It was necessary, therefore, not merely to abolish the old, but to give detailed reasons for changes.

Most of the work on the constitution was Condorcet's.

In committee, Paine's lack of fluency in French was far more of a drawback than it was in the Convention, though in any case he was too intemperate to be a good committee man. The draft constitution, however, was all labor lost. Robespierre and his friends, who were not on the committee, perceived that they would have more power in the present Convention than in a new Assembly elected on a system drawn up by their foes. They accordingly succeeded in postponing discussion until the fate of King Louis should be decided.

The death of Louis XVI was desired by the Jacobins, partly out of sheer hatred of kings, but far more ardently for current political reasons. The ghastly massacres of September had rallied those who shuddered at such crimes behind the Girondists, who had been waging an ill-concealed war against the Jacobins ever since. Thus even before the arrival of Paine, the French republicans had split into factions. The death of Louis, if consented to by the Girondists, would sever connections between them and the moderates forever, cutting the ground from under their feet and driving them into the arms of the extremists.

Circumstances favored the Jacobins. Under the auspices of the Girondists, the war against Austria was now going miraculously well. The enemy had left French soil and Belgium had been occupied. But the Convention, drunk with victory, was easily persuaded that it could afford to defy the world. Indeed, convinced, in part through Paine, that the slightest push would cause an English revolution, it dared to threaten England, who was becoming anxious about the fate of Belgium and Holland.

Such a mood led naturally to violent measures. Meanwhile, an iron chest had been discovered in the Tuileries

containing papers which revealed the intrigues of the
Court against the Revolution. Their publication aroused
feelings against Louis to boiling point. Some of the papers
implicated public figures, so that suspicion ran riot, and
any moderate risked being called a secret traitor. Even
the Girondists were forced for the sake of appearances to
be severe.

With nice calculation, the Jacobins sponsored a movement for putting Louis to death as a public enemy without a formal trial. Thus the Girondists, who had proposed
a plebiscite because they knew the country as a whole was
disposed to be lenient, were forced to concede that he
should be tried before the Convention. This point gained,
the Jacobins had their enemies in a trap. The galleries of
the Convention were daily packed with the toughest characters of the Paris mob. These were the people who had
devoured the heart of the Princesse de Lamballe, shot
her mangled limbs out of cannons, and performed other
acts upon her body even more monstrous. As one of the
Girondists described them: "It seemed as if their leaders
had sought in all the slums of Paris and Europe for everything that was most hideous and polluted. With dreadful
earthen faces black or copper-colored, with eyes half-
sunken in their sockets, they gave vent with fetid breath to
the coarsest insults and the shrill screams of hungry ani-
mals." To oppose such creatures on the floor of the Convention was not much safer than walking into a den of
hungry lions. In the circumstances, the condemnation of
the King was a foregone conclusion.

It remained to debate his punishment, but the Girondists were beginning to panic and had become split over
the issue. Again they desired a plebiscite, but the galleries

which dominated the Convention were not willing to permit the decision to be made elsewhere.

It is typical of Paine that at the moment when the party of the Gironde was struggling for its existence, he voted against it. It is fair to say that the Girondists themselves were confused. In the matter of the life or death of the King, any man might be likely to consult his own conscience sooner than his party. All the same, when Paine voted against a plebiscite, he was acting precisely as he always had done. His inability to compromise with other points of view might make him a valuable critic of outworn traditions, but it unfitted him to understand political maneuvers which relied on party loyalty. Besides, his far-from-fluent French cut him off from understanding those who would not take especial pains to talk with him.

After voting against his best friends, Paine now proceeded with his usual lack of caution to offend the Jacobins. The voting on the King's fate began at eight in the evening in a dim assembly hall in which only the tribune on which men mounted to give their verdicts was brightly lit. It took real courage to stand there in full sight of the bloodthirsty galleries and utter any word but "death."

Courage of this sort Paine had; besides he had nailed his colors to the mast a few days earlier by handing in a paper to be published with the proceedings of the Convention. He did not hesitate now to repeat his recommendations: imprisonment for the King until the end of the war, and banishment thereafter.

The majority vote was for death, but a number of people who had not dared to follow Paine's example had salved their consciences by recommending the Convention grant a reprieve in the public interest. Thus another debate took place, during which Paine received permission to be heard.

He walked up to the platform with a close friend, who was to read the French translation of his manuscript. The enthusiasm which had greeted his appearance only a few months before had disappeared. No sooner had Paine's opening words been read, regretting the death verdict of the previous day, than Marat jumped up.

"I deny the right of Thomas Paine to vote on such a subject, as he is a Quaker; hence his religious views run counter to the infliction of capital punishment."

Of all the extremists in the Convention, Marat was at this time the most terrifying figure. Haggard, with burning eyes, his pallid face disfigured with running sores, Marat posed as the incarnation of the Paris slums, affecting a red bandanna tied around his head, ragged costume, and sockless feet thrust into dirty boots. "I am the rage of the people," he cried of himself. His paper, *L'Ami du Peuple,* called for bloodshed in the most ferocious terms, while the September massacres were known to have been largely his work. What Paine thought when he found such a man prominent in the Convention which was to usher in the golden age is unclear. Certainly he blamed the old regime for having produced him, but he must have perceived the signs of future trouble.

There was uproar in the Assembly as Marat's followers applauded him, while other deputies shouted for freedom of speech. After a while, the reading continued. Paine argued that the execution of the King would be interpreted by royalists abroad as vengeance, not justice. In particular, the United States, sole friend to the Revolution, would be alienated by the death of a ruler who had contributed so largely to their own freedom.

Once more Marat sprang to his feet. These were not Paine's real opinions. The translator had perverted them, and Paine did not understand what was being read.

Loudly Paine protested that he did. This was January, and he had been in France since the previous September, besides spending many months in the country previously.

A third time Marat interrupted, shouting once more that Paine had voted against the death penalty as a Quaker. Paine denied it. He had been influenced only by regard for the public interest and for morality.

His courage was not matched by the rest of the Convention. Even royalists agreed that the most powerful effort made in the Convention to save Louis from death was that of Paine. Brissot, the Girondist leader, actually voted for death; and most of his principal followers did the same. They would not risk their lives or political futures to save Louis, not perceiving that they were in any case doomed once they had ceased to be leaders. As for Paine, he might have found a threat in Robespierre's report on his speech, which recorded "The part of the assembly where the warmest patriots were seated began to murmur in protest."

Two days later, on the twenty-first of January, Louis was executed. On the surface, the Girondists were still leaders of the nation, but throughout the next two months their position grew weaker. Dumouriez, their general in Brussels, was in great difficulties, partly because the Belgians were losing their illusions about the Revolution, and partly because the minister of war was secretly in league with Marat, who desired a defeat to discredit the Girondists. No supplies reached Dumouriez, who finally followed the example of Lafayette and deserted to the Austrians. Meanwhile, on February 1, the Convention had added to its problems by declaring war against England, which did not forthwith break out in revolution.

The misfortunes of their army might not be the fault of the Girondists, but in fact they showed no aptitude for war. Danton's was the voice which aroused the nation, but the Girondists disdained to seek his help, preferring to drive him into the ranks of their enemies.

Mismanagement led to rumors of treachery, and Danton stampeded the Convention into appointing a Revolutionary Tribunal to try the enemies of the people. This dangerous body had hardly been set up when the news of Dumouriez's defection reached Paris. Already it was evident that a body of over seven hundred led by windy speakers and unhampered by effective rules of procedure was incapable of ruling the nation. In the atmosphere of excitement which followed the general's desertion, extremists had things their own way. A Committee of Public Safety was created with wide executive powers, and among its members there was not a single Girondist. Immediately it started to examine the papers of Girondist ministers.

The Girondists struck back as best they could. Marat, now president of the Jacobin club, was using his position to denounce the Girondists to the affiliated clubs throughout the provinces. A counterrevolution impended, he warned. Let the people rise, pillage the shops of suspected merchants and hang the proprietors over their doors. The Convention was riddled with traitors and its incompetence would soon force the nation to abolish democracy. His circular was read to the Convention, and the Girondists charged Marat with inciting pillage and murder and with plotting to overthrow the sovereignty of the people. The Convention, outraged at Marat's description of itself, which was indeed only too true, decreed his arrest and trial before the Revolutionary Tribunal.

It was one thing to arrest Marat, quite another to condemn him. The Revolutionary Tribunal, packed with agents of the Paris Commune, was eager to show the Convention who was master. There is no doubt that on one pretext or another Marat would have been acquitted. His guilt, however, was so obvious that his supporters felt the need of a diversion. Eagerly they seized on an incident which occurred at this time.

Paine had changed his living quarters to an apartment which he shared with a couple of Englishmen, William Choppin and a young doctor, William Johnson. The apartment was not elaborate. It consisted of a room for utilities —wood, water, and clothes closet; a bedroom; and a pleasant sitting room which looked into the garden. Outside were ducks and turkeys, geese, rabbits, a pigsty and a well-stocked orchard with a kitchen garden.

William Johnson, who was obviously neurotic, developed an idea that Marat was plotting against Paine's life. Johnson's reaction to this threat to his friend was to commit suicide. He made a will dividing his possessions between Choppin and Paine and added a statement that he came to France to enjoy liberty, but found it had been assassinated by Marat. He could not endure the triumph of "imbecillity and inhumanity" over "talent and virtue." Having set the scene, he stabbed himself twice, called to Choppin, and thrust the declaration into his hands, gasping that he had killed himself. When Paine, too, came rushing in,

Johnson took a solemn farewell and gave him his watch.

Ludicrously, it turned out that Johnson was not even badly wounded. Paine, however, showed the declaration to Brissot, who published it with the explanation that an Englishman who had come to France to find liberty had decided to kill himself when he found "only its mask on the hideous visage of anarchy." Before dying, said Brissot, he wrote "with his trembling hand" this accusation of Marat "on a paper now in the hands of an eminent foreigner."

Brissot's unscrupulous tactics were his undoing. The prosecutors decided to accuse Marat of causing Johnson's breakdown, through the pernicious effect of his writings. Thus when Marat came before the Revolutionary Tribunal, his friends were able to confine the case almost entirely to this incident.

Paine was naturally called as a witness and had to admit that he had only spoken to Marat once in his life, on casually meeting him in the hall of the Convention. Marat had declared that the English were free and happy, while Paine had replied they were groaning under tyranny. Anyone could see that it was hardly likely that Marat had singled out Paine and threatened his life.

Questioned on this point, Johnson attributed his action to having read that Marat had said all those who voted for an appeal to the people in the trial of Louis should be massacred. As it happened, Paine had not so voted; and in any case the general statement hardly suggested a personal threat. Meanwhile English friends agreed that Johnson had long been showing signs of mental breakdown.

The defense merely had to maintain that Marat's words could hardly be called serious treason just because they influenced neurotic people. The jury hastened to acquit

him. He was immediately surrounded by his yelling supporters, who snatched his red handkerchief off and re-
placed it with a crown of laurel. In this guise they chaired
him to the Convention, smashed open the door in the
middle of the session, and bore him in. After a few triumph-
ant words, he was carried off again to the Jacobin Club,
real center of power, and enthroned in the president's
seat.

Such scenes were by now not unusual in the Convention. At any hour of the day, raucous delegations burst
in with demands, which were hastily granted because most
of the deputies were terrified men and the rest in collusion.
In reply, the Girondists, now fully aware of their danger,
could think of nothing more practical than to appoint a
committee charged to look into things.

Meanwhile, Paine found another chance to attract the
enmity of those who could do him harm. General Fran-
cisco Miranda, a South American revolutionary and
friend of Paine's, had been principal subordinate to Dumouriez and defeated with him in the course of the campaign against Holland and Belgium. He was brought to
trial for treason, and Paine gave evidence for him, stating
that Miranda had defended human liberty in America,
England, and France, that the first object of his heart was
the deliverance of Spanish America, and that he was incapable of conspiring with the Austrians. Miranda was
acquitted, and the deluded Girondists began to believe that
they had not lost their power.

The defense of Miranda was characteristic of Paine, one
of whose virtues was fidelity to friends in trouble and even
generosity to enemies. Early in the year he had got into an
argument at White's with a British naval captain, who

struck him and very nearly knocked him off his chair. Striking a Deputy was an insult to the French nation and punishable by death. It caused Paine a good deal of difficulty to obtain the man's release from the Committee of Public Safety.

The fall of the Girondists was now imminent. In vain did Paine draw up an appeal to Danton as the only man who could save the state from the spirit of faction. Despairing of the French Revolution, he wrote to America that he was coming home; but he was soon to find that he had no power to do so. The National Guard was now commanded by a creature of the Commune, Hanriot, already implicated in the September massacres. On May 31, when Paine appeared at the gate of the Tuileries, where the Convention was sitting, Hanriot stopped him from going in. When Paine showed his Deputy's card, Hanriot rudely told him that he could use it to make curl-papers with. Danton, who was just coming out of the hall, warned Paine in English not to go in, lest he be denounced together with his friends.

Paine quoted a friend who had said that the French Revolution was devouring its own children, but Danton merely shrugged.

"Revolutions cannot be made with rose water," said he.

For a few days the Girondists saved themselves at the price of sacrificing their new committee. Barère, President of the Convention, tried to persuade them to resign their offices and relinquish power; but this they refused. On the second of June, surrounded by detachments of the National Guard and menaced by roars of a mob without and screams and threats of the extremists within, the Convention was forced to expel twenty-two Girondist leaders and decree their arrest. Some Deputies escaped to the provinces, where many cities already chafed under the rule of the Jacobins. A royalist revolt had broken out, and the appeals of the Girondists now added to the confusion. France seemed to be breaking apart, but tyranny clamped down all the harder on Paris.

1793-94
The Terror

The fall and arrest of the Girondists put Paine in imminent danger. It was clear to all that their deaths would soon follow. Indeed, one of their leaders had screamed across the floor of the Convention at a friend of Robespierre's, "Give Couthon his glass of blood!" as he was hustled away.

Paine himself, it is true, was not precisely a Girondist. Indeed, his chief protection lay in the fact that as a foreigner and an outsider, he was politically powerless. In addition, as long as the Revolution cared for its reputation abroad, his fame must defend him. Yet there was a danger in this, too, lest he be suspected of turning his talents against the Revolution.

In the Convention itself, he was now completely silenced. None of his remaining friends dared translate his papers into French or read them aloud. Yet his absence from this body might be interpreted as dangerous sympathy with the Girondists. On the whole, he found it his wisest course to attend occasionally, choosing moments when nothing important was going on. "I found it impossible," he later explained, "to join in their tremendous decrees and useless and dangerous to oppose them."

In the evenings of that spring and summer he paced up and down the garden amid the ducks and geese which he

had liked in happier days to feed from his window. There
was much on his mind. Should he, for instance, return to
America while he could get safely away, or had he a duty
as Deputy to remain? After the arrest of the Girondists,
Calais sent an address to the Convention, strongly condemning the conduct of Paine in supporting them. If he
had lost the confidence of his constituents, was there any
need to represent them further?

In his usual fashion, Paine wavered, now despairing
utterly of France, and now regaining his faith that good
must come from Revolution. There were at this time
American ships at Bordeaux, seized by the French because
they had been carrying goods to England. The captains of
these vessels had appealed in vain to Gouverneur Morris,
now American minister and totally out of sympathy with
the Revolution. He merely answered that they had put
themselves into the lion's mouth and would have to get
out of it as best they could. Perhaps this had been an out-
burst of temper concealing the fact that it was unlikely
the Jacobins would listen to his protests. At all events,
Morris did point out to the French Minister for Foreign
Affairs that ill-treatment of Americans would put an end
to trade with France. Meanwhile, however, the captains
themselves had turned to Paine for help.

Paine applied to Barère, who had kept his position as
President of the Convention at the price of bowing to the
dictatorship of the Committee of Public Safety and endorsing the decrees which established the Terror. Despite
his failings, Barère was efficient and by no means personally malicious. He was ready to be on good terms with
Paine as long as the latter was tolerated by those in power.
Accordingly, he spoke to Paine one day when he met him

in the street, took him into the Foreign Ministry to find an interpreter, and asked his advice on sending commissioners to America to seek an alliance in the war against England.

Paine was all enthusiasm, since whatever he might think of France at the present moment, he was convinced that the real enemy to the Revolution of the world was the government of England. He told Barère that he would not serve personally as a commissioner, even though he planned to return to America at the end of the year. His fellow countrymen, and indeed he himself preferred he should do so as an American, not as a Frenchman. Nevertheless his advice and support would be forthcoming to the fullest possible extent.

This was satisfactory to Barère, who valued Paine's co-operation but thought him not sufficiently smooth in manner for an envoy. Let him devote his talents to making the French popular among the American people. There was general understanding between Paine and Barère that as soon as the captains detained in Bordeaux were released, he would sail for America with them.

In the meantime, there was much that Paine could do for France in getting timely American aid. He worked long hours in the Bureau of Foreign Affairs, advising methods of approach, overseeing correspondence, and generally applying his personal knowledge of Americans and their affairs. Important grain shipments came over as a result in the following year, but by that time Paine was in prison.

It is not clear why Paine changed his mind about sailing in October when the American vessels set out. Perhaps he discovered they were going home by way of England, where he dared not return. Perhaps he was warned that he would be arrested if he tried to go. At all events, his decision cannot have been due to optimism about the course of events in France, for October saw the death of Marie Antoinette and of the imprisoned Girondists. By a law passed in September, every citizen who was not granted a pass by his local revolutionary committee was automatically subject to arrest. There were hideous massacres in the provinces as cities which had thrown off the Jacobin rule were brought to heel. In Paris, the guillotine was set up permanently; and trials before the Revolutionary Tribunal became a farce.

The Committee of Public Safety, now led by Robespierre, was exterminating those whose birth, or talents, or political connections might make them leaders of an opposition. There were many on whom the green eyes of Robespierre rested with an ominous suspicion. They included Danton, his uneasy ally, and the Paris Commune which had swept the Girondists out of power. By comparison with these, Paine mattered little; but the Terror imperiled the obscure as well as the powerful. In any case, he had great abilities which might prove dangerous.

He was attacked for the first time in October as one of the seventy-three who had voted against the arrest of the Girondists in March. In fact, he was singled out by name as an Englishman, thus clearly an enemy, and one who had not scrupled to threaten France with the displeasure of the United States, her natural ally, over the execution of the tyrant Louis. This denunciation, though made in the name of the Committee of Public Safety, proved premature. Robespierre himself took the floor to say that not all the seventy-three were necessarily guilty. Indeed this was almost three weeks before the Girondist leaders were tried and executed. For the present there was no further motion to attack Paine.

He had been reprieved, but not for long. "I saw many of my most intimate friends destroyed," he wrote, "others daily carried to prison, and I had reason to believe, and had also intimations given me that the same danger was approaching myself."

The continuance of the war was arousing nationalist feeling. Paine did not consider himself an Englishman, but his imperfect French and the company he kept were enough to convict him. Choppin and Johnson had already fled the country soon after the acquittal of Marat. Two nights after they were gone, Paine heard a knocking at the gate. Looking out of his bedroom window in night-cap and gown, he saw the landlord going out with a candle and watched him unlock the gate for a guard with muskets and fixed bayonets. With a sinking heart he got back to bed, resigning himself to arrest and prison. To his relief, they were only after Choppin and Johnson. About a month later, they came again and took away the landlord. Paine was left alone in the house awaiting his turn.

It is at this time, say his friends, that Paine truly despaired and began to drink heavily. The loss of the high hopes with which he had come to France, the danger and destruction of his friends, and the threat of arrest which hung over him were ample excuse. However this may be, he did not drown his abilities in brandy. On the contrary, he made up his mind to appeal once more to the public. Brooding over the desperate course which the French Revolution had taken, he followed a line of thought not unlike Burke's. By sweeping away moral and religious standards, the French had opened the door to every excess. In his attachment to the past, however, Burke had offered no suggestion about what should be done. He had merely indulged in gloomy prophecies, now being fulfilled. To Paine's very different mind, a fresh interpretation of the facts presented itself. The fault actually lay with the Church, which had bred intolerance and persecution. Since the influence of the Church had waned, these qualities had simply transferred themselves to politics, where they were raging unchecked because nobody had introduced a rational faith or system of morals.

What ought to be the faith of an intelligent man? Was it not possible to lay out a new foundation on which the brotherhood of mankind could be erected? *The Age of Reason* is Paine's last great message to his time, and it concerns itself with even more fundamental ideas than *The Rights of Man*.

On Christmas Day, which was no longer celebrated in France, Robespierre made an ominous speech to the frightened Convention, making mention of strangers in their midst who lacked true sympathy with the principles of the Revolution. This was amplified by Barère, who was by now afraid for himself and did not hesitate to curry favor by attacking Paine directly. In his sympathies, proclaimed Barère, Paine was a Girondist who had not set foot in the Convention since the expulsion of Brissot. Furthermore, Barère knew that Paine was currently intriguing with a former agent of the Ministry of Foreign Affairs. In hasty response, the Convention decreed that no foreigner could be admitted to represent the French people.

Paine's arrest was now clearly a matter of days. He

worked hard to make the last corrections on *The Age of Reason*, which he duly finished on the evening of December 27. That night he supped at White's, now for patriotic reasons the Hotel de Philadelphie, in company with some Americans. They sat up talking till midnight, so that Paine, whose lodgings were a mile and a half away, took a bed for the night. Between three and four in the morning he was awakened by the guard sent to arrest him, which had traced him to the hotel. Two officers of the Committee came with them to check his papers.

Paine got up, dressed, and asked the guards to escort him to the room of Achille Audibert, the friend from Calais who had persuaded him to join the Convention. Through Audibert as interpreter, he informed the commissioners that his friend Joel Barlow had part of a manuscript of his which was being printed.

This was true, since Barlow lived near the printer and had agreed to pick up the proofs of the first half of *The Age of Reason*. In any case, however, Paine desired the presence of an American at the examination of his papers. He wanted, moreover, to give Barlow the second half of *The Age of Reason*, which he had just completed.

By eight o'clock the commissioners came to the conclusion that Paine was merely playing for time by visiting Barlow. Worn out by a sleepless night, they agreed to take rest and refreshment, but after this they insisted on visiting Paine's apartment. Here they spent four or five hours looking through his papers, but could find nothing more suspicious than a manuscript written for the Committee of Public Safety on commerce between the United States and France. They drew up a favorable report and signed

it, then escorted Paine to the Luxembourg prison, allowing him to drop off *The Age of Reason* with Barlow on
the way.

Paine's friends immediately rallied to present a petition for his release signed by sixteen Americans. It pointed
out that Paine had been invited to France by the French
people and that none would be more pleased at his arrest than the government of England. His papers had ad-
mittedly contained nothing treasonable. Claiming him as
an American citizen, the signers offered surety for his
conduct until he could return to his own country.

The reply which they received was unrelenting: Paine
was born an Englishman, which alone was sufficient to
make his arrest legal. Moreover, though he might have
done noble things in the American Revolution, he had
not comprehended the nature of the Revolution which had
regenerated France. He had made common cause with
its false friends, so that it would have been more fitting
for Americans to deplore his errors than to petition for
his freedom.

With such an answer, nothing could be done; but the
names on the petition had been remarkable for one omis-
sion. Gouverneur Morris, American minister to France,
had not signed it. Whether he had been approached to do
so is uncertain, but in any case it was now necessary for
Paine to turn to him.

Gouverneur Morris was in a difficult position, and views
to this day differ about the fairness of his behavior to
Paine. Paine's argument naturally was that as a citizen
of the United States he could not commit treason against
France. In support of this he could point out that he had
been arrested mainly on the ground that he was a

foreigner. On the other hand, he was also an honorary
citizen of France. Paine contended that Washington,
Priestley, and others had been made citizens by the same
decree, which had been the merest compliment, in no way
interfering with the nationalities of those whom it distinguished. His enemies replied that none of the others had
accepted a seat in the National Convention or resided in
France.

Gouverneur Morris, who hated the French Revolution
from the bottom of his heart, had always disliked and
distrusted Paine. Long ago in Philadelphia they had first
disagreed. He was deeply indignant when Paine began interfering in French affairs, which were in Morris' view
none of his business. In addition, Paine's earlier attempts
to become unofficial minister to England, or even to
France, had brought him into rivalry with Morris, who
had by now succeeded to both offices. He must, presumably, have been aware of Paine's most recent efforts to
mediate between America and France. When Commissioners were actually sent to America in the following
year, their first act was to press for Morris' recall. In any
case, nothing could be further from Gouverneur Morris'
wishes than that the United States should ally itself with
the French Revolution.

For all these reasons, the relationship between the two
men was thoroughly embittered. What made the matter
worse was that Morris conscientiously felt that Paine's behavior in France had amounted to a change in citizenship.
In fact, Paine had made his bed, and now he did not want
to lie on it. Visibly pleased with the situation, Morris reported in the following terms to Thomas Jefferson, now
Secretary of State:

"Lest I should forget it, I must mention that Thomas Paine is in prison, where he amuses himself with publishing a pamphlet against Jesus Christ. I do not recollect whether I mentioned to you that he would have been executed along with the rest of the Brissotins if the advance party had not viewed him with contempt. I incline to think that if he is quiet in prison he may have the good luck to be forgotten, whereas, should he be brought much into notice, the long-suspended axe might fall on him. I believe he thinks that I ought to claim him as an American citizen; but considering his birth, his naturalization in this country, and the place that he filled, I doubt very much the right, and I am sure that the claim would be, for the present at least, inexpedient and ineffectual."

Morris had a right to form his own opinions and to advise the Secretary of State. He may even have been correct in supposing that Paine's best policy was to lie low for a while and hope to be forgotten. It is clear, however, from the whole tone of this letter that his conclusions had been colored by prejudice. It was hard on Paine to have his fate depend on a man who could write of him with such unfeeling contempt. The prison in which he found himself was constantly being emptied by the guillotine and filled again to overflowing by people often far less prominent than he. Obscurity did not save them. It was only natural that Paine should try and insist that Morris take action.

Morris gave way, at least to some extent. American or not, Paine was a person to whom his country owed a great deal. Accordingly, he wrote to the Minister for Foreign Affairs as follows:

"Thomas Paine has just applied to me to claim him as a Citizen of the United States. These (I believe) are the facts which relate to him. He was born in England. Becoming subsequently a citizen of the United States, he there acquired a great celebrity through his revolutionary writings. In consequence he was adopted as a French citizen and then elected a Member of the Convention. His conduct since that period is out of my jurisdiction. I am ignorant of the reason for his present detention in the Luxembourg prison, but I beg you (if there are reasons unknown to me which prevent his liberation) please be so good as to inform me of them, so that I may communicate them to the government of the United States."

Even allowing for diplomatic prose, one can hardly feel that this letter was likely to accomplish anything. Morris refrains from claiming Paine as an American, does not defend his conduct, and does not urge his release. He evidently felt that he had no right to do any of these things. The Foreign Minister took his hint and replied that in accepting French citizenship Paine had renounced the protection of the United States. The Minister did not know why he had been arrested, but would pass the letter of inquiry on to the Committee of Public Safety.

The lack of enthusiasm felt by Morris was conveyed in another report to Jefferson, stating that Paine had desired him to claim him as an American citizen, and that he had complied against his better judgment. He enclosed the answer of the Minister for Foreign Affairs, of which he had sent Paine a copy. An unknown Englishman had turned up in Morris' office with a long reply to the Minister, written by Paine, which he wished Morris to copy and send. Morris had retorted that he quite agreed with the Minister's argument. Moreover, if the authorities wished to release Paine, they now had a pretext. If they did not, it might be dangerous to bring on his trial. "I have heard no more of the matter since," he concluded, "but it is not impossible that he may force on a decision, which, as far as I can judge, would be fatal to him: for in the best of times he has a larger share of every other sense than common sense, and lately the intemperate use of ardent spirits has, I am told, considerably impaired the small stock he originally possessed."

If Paine was still drinking deeply, he had cause. The Luxembourg prison had been a palace and still preserved an atmosphere of faded splendor. Its elderly keeper, Benoit, was genuinely kind and made an effort to place each prisoner in a group which would be congenial. Since the Luxembourg was the prison to which many English prisoners were sent, Paine did not lack companions he could talk to. During the daytime, prisoners went in and out of their rooms as they pleased, doing their own cooking and associating in small groups. There were, however, many discomforts due to crowded conditions or hasty regulations imposed on the prison.

Paine had a room on the ground floor, level with the garden and paved with brick. It was so wet after every rain that he was continually catching cold. Though he had money, fuel was difficult and candles impossible to obtain. Presently Benoit, who had been especially kind to Paine, was arrested himself. An order was given to seize the prisoners' knives, forks, and sharp instruments to prevent their cheating the guillotine by suicide. Some money was confiscated too; and Paine took the lock off his door and hid some gold coins and a large bank note inside it. Cash was necessary, as the prisoners had to pay for their board and a barber to shave them. Expenses, however, were kept to a modest sum, while the duration of prisoners' stay in the place grew constantly shorter.

Over all hung the shadow of the guillotine. By now a trial was simply a farce of a few minutes' duration, followed by a ride in a cart to the place of execution. In the place of those who were disposed of, fresh arrivals brought news from outside of the rising of the Terror. Among these at the end of March came Danton, hurried to the scaffold because those who hated him also feared his strength. "What you have done for the happiness and liberty of your country, I have in vain tried to do for mine," he said to Paine. "I have been less fortunate, but not more guilty."

Danton died, but Paine still lived. Was it possible that Morris had been right and he was forgotten? The inhabitants of the Luxembourg were like a flock of sheep waiting for the butcher. Every night the guards came round for victims, and every morning the tumbrils set out for the guillotine. Spies scattered through the prison reported casual words or nervous outbursts as signs of conspiracy and speeded the suspects on their way to death.

The strain of confinement under unhealthy conditions may have saved Paine's life by bringing on a fever which almost killed him. He thought himself on his deathbed; but so far from being terrified at having offended his Maker by the composition of *The Age of Reason,* he experienced relief and satisfaction at having left his opinions on religion to mankind. Luckily for him he was removed to a better room and devotedly nursed by his three fellow inmates, Joseph Vanhuele, Charles Bastinit, and Michael Rubyns, all Belgians. Besides the prison physician, there were two English doctors among the prisoners, so that he had constant attention. He survived, but barely, hardly conscious of what was going on for nearly eight weeks. When he came to himself again and looked about him, some three hundred of his fellow prisoners were gone forever. A memorandum was later found in Robespierre's papers demanding the condemnation of Paine, which probably was postponed on account of this illness.

Paine tells us that an attempt was later made to include him among the victims of the guillotine. On one night in July, a hundred and sixty-eight were removed from the Luxembourg for trial and execution. It was the practice of the people in charge to go through the prison in the evening and mark with chalk on each door how many were to be taken. It happened, however, that Paine's door was under a balcony and had been left wide open against the wall. Thus those who came to mark it for death wrote "4" on the inside instead of the outside, not noticing in the gloom of the place what they were doing. Nor did Paine and his friends, going candleless to bed, discover the fatal sign until next morning.

This accident would not have saved Paine for long, since the spies in the prison must soon have reported that he was still alive. But two days after this event, the Terror came to a sudden end with the fall of Robespierre. The prisoners, though they were not sure of it at first, were saved. Paine's head remained on his shoulders, but he had yet to find a way of getting free.

1794-96
Reason and Unreason

A French translation of *The Age of Reason* was published in July, 1794, about a week after Robespierre died on the guillotine. The circumstance suggests that Paine and his friends did not dare attract attention earlier. This was wise, since the pamphlet once more caused an international sensation. True to his usual habits, Paine was forcible in stating his opinions.

"I believe in one God and no more; and I hope for happiness beyond this life," he explains.

"I believe in the equality of man; and I believe that religious duties consist in doing justice, loving mercy, and endeavoring to make our fellow-creatures happy."

"I do not believe in the creed professed by the Jewish Church, by the Roman Church, by the Greek Church, by the Turkish Church, by the Protestant Church, nor by any church that I know of. My own mind is my own church."

Paine has, in fact, a particular hatred for churches, which he regards as institutions set up to enslave mankind for their own profit. They are, he believes, maintained by mental lies which produce grave moral mischief. Men are deliberately taught to believe in propositions which in any other department of life they would not accept. This is done by Christians, Jews, and Mohammedans alike on the authority of revelations made directly by God. With this preliminary, Paine proceeds to tear the Christian religion to shreds.

A revelation from God, he points out, is only a revelation to the actual person who receives it. To those who learn it at secondhand, it is but hearsay. The Virgin Birth and the Annunciation, for instance, were revealed directly to no one but Joseph and Mary. Paine sees no reason why he should accept so improbable a story on the authority of interested parties. In similar fashion, the truth of the Resurrection was only directly known by eight or nine persons. Why should the rest of the world be called on to believe it without evidence? "It appears that Thomas did not believe the resurrection, and as they say, would not believe without having ocular and manual demonstration himself. *So neither will I.*"

He is ready to admit that he intends no disrespect to the character of Jesus. "He was a virtuous and an amiable man. The morality that he preached and practised was of the most benevolent kind; and though similar systems of morality had been preached by Confucius, and by some of the Greek philosophers, many years before; by the Quakers since; and by many good men in all ages, it has not been exceeded by any." This is sincere praise and yet Paine's reduction of Jesus to human scale was meant to be offensive.

Having thus disposed of the pretensions of Jesus, Paine finds it easy to be witty about the beliefs which Christians inherited from the Jewish scriptures. He is, in particular, outraged by the legend of the expulsion of Satan from heaven and his corruption of Adam and Eve in the Garden of Eden. Is it not an insult to the power of God that He should not have been able to control the Evil One better? The Devil is a pure invention of the makers of the Christian legend, who found him useful. "They promised him ALL the Jews, ALL the Turks by anticipation, nine-tenths of the world beside, and Mahomet into the bargain. After this, who can doubt the bountifulness of the Christian Mythology."

Reviewing the Bible as a whole, Paine despises the Old Testament because of its stories of vindictive cruelty. He dismisses the Prophets as poets, not more inspired than any others. He admires the Book of Job and some of the Psalms and Proverbs, contending, however, that a small amount of lofty writing is insufficient reason for calling the whole book the Word of God. In the New Testament, as we have seen, he does admire Jesus, but has been since childhood revolted by the doctrine of the atonement preached by St. Paul.

The effect on human character of this curious hodge-podge of beliefs is, he imagines, disastrous. Man is taught to despise himself and, what is worse, to despise the world created by God. God's choicest gift to man, the gift of reason, is dismissed in favor of divine revelation. At the same time, man is encouraged in extraordinary presumption. "He takes on himself to direct the Almighty what to do, even in the government of the universe; he prays dictatorially; when it is sunshine, he prays for rain; he follows the same idea in everything he prays for; for what is the amount of all his prayers but an attempt to make the Almighty change His mind, and act otherwise than He does? It is as if he were to say: Thou knowest not so well as I."

What then is God and what is true religion? God is the Creator, and His revelation to man is the universe we live in. The instrument by which we perceive this and apprehend the greatness of God is human reason. In other words, it is through science that we come to know God. Science discovers the principles by which the world is regulated and governed. We find these are orderly, wise, sensible, even benevolent, since they preserve the harmony of the universe. We are encouraged to become the same. The more we know, the more our reason tells us that these are the qualities God demands of us.

Now whether it is really possible to deduce a moral duty to treat men as equals or to love mercy from what science tells us about the way the world is run, Paine's religion does reflect the views of many thoughtful men of his times. They believed, as he did, in a personal God, the Creator, who is to be seen in His works and understood by reason. Deism, as such beliefs were called, is not original with Paine, but is a product of the excitement generated by the development of experimental science. In essence, it was the faith of Franklin, Jefferson, and most of the intellectuals of Europe. It is embodied in a famous hymn which Paine quotes with approval, representing the manner in which the stars of the universe praise God.

> "In reason's ear they all rejoice
> And utter forth a glorious voice,
> Forever singing as they shine,
> THE HAND THAT MADE US IS DIVINE."

This being the case, it was not really Paine's religion, but what he did not believe that made him notorious. Christianity has changed a great deal since Paine's day, as a result of that very science he so admired. It is, for instance, no longer possible for most Christians to accept a Creation which took place in seven days or to believe in the expulsion of Adam and Eve from the Garden of Eden. Other doctrines have been indirectly affected, so that Christians can be found who do not believe in a personal Devil, or even in angels, or in hell. Some are skeptical about the Virgin Birth, and others about the doctrine of the Atonement. In other words, though it may be necessary to hold particular doctrines in order to belong to a particular church, those accepted by every Christian have greatly decreased. Paine's ridicule of Christian beliefs is bound to seem less shocking in an age when many of them are not regarded as essential. To understand the strength of feeling against him, we have to think ourselves back to days when doctrine was rigid.

Paine's criticisms, to be sure, were no more original than his science. As usual, it was the frank way in which he expressed them that roused the public. Learned commentaries might point out contradictions in the Bible to scholars. Benjamin Franklin might discuss his inmost feelings with men of a like mind some quiet evening. No one but Paine thought it necessary to drop a bombshell in the very midst of the congregation.

Its impact was shattering. Paine's following in England contained a large proportion of nonconformists, not the less strict in religion because they hated the established church. The change in opinion there may be illustrated by the fact that Thomas Erskine, who in 1792 had defended Paine's right to publish *The Rights of Man,* now conducted the government's prosecution of *The Age of Reason.* In America, where Paine's admirers included many pious people of the New England states, *The Age of Reason* was widely greeted with horror. Only in France was

Paine acceptable, at least to the ruling cliques, but for a reason which he himself deplored. He had written his pamphlet to combat atheism, which he saw spreading widely among the leaders of the French Revolution; but his arguments against Christianity proved more powerful than his positive creed.

Thus at a stroke Paine demolished his reputation. His followers had especially included the poor or the half-educated, the common man groping for political freedom. It was his misfortune that religious freedom was not desired by the same group. From this time onward, a new venom was added to the attack upon him. A general feeling was current that Thomas Paine had sold his soul to the Devil.

His immediate problem was to get out of prison, and neither he nor his friends were backward in seeking his release. Lanthenas, the translator of *The Age of Reason,* sent an early copy with his appeal to the Committee of Public Safety. Achille Audibert, ever faithful, wrote also. Paine himself directed one appeal to the Committee, and a second to the Convention. Though executions were at an end, however, nobody seemed ready to take the initiative in opening the prisons. It was lucky that, about the middle of August, 1794, Gouverneur Morris, who had made no further effort for Paine, was superseded as minister by James Monroe, an admirer and personal friend.

Paine immediately addressed a letter to Monroe, followed by another when he did not receive an answer at once. He had now been eight months in prison, and his health was seriously affected. Since his fever, he had developed an abcess in his side which would not heal. Understandably, he had lost all patience.

Monroe still failed to answer Paine, no doubt because he was seeking advice. Paine's was no more than a small piece of unfinished business left over by Gouverneur Morris, whose opinion was that Paine had no right to official help. A report got around to Paine that he was not to be considered an American citizen, and he frantically sent Monroe a forty-three-page manuscript upon the subject.

Finally, on September 18, Monroe wrote him a warm and generous letter, declaring that "By being with us through the revolution, you are of our country as absolutely as if you had been born there."

Paine responded gratefully, but nine days later when his imprisonment did not come to an end, he began to wonder whether Monroe really meant what he said. Perhaps he wanted him to be freed in the course of events without official intervention. Perhaps he was relying on promises from influential Frenchmen whom he did not yet fully know. These dark suspicions were intolerable, and Paine despatched another letter.

A month went by. To Monroe, proceeding cautiously to sound out people who did not like to commit themselves, the business of effecting Paine's release was a delicate one. He had been sent over to establish good relations with the government of France, so it did not suit him to make an official demand if it would be rebuffed. To Paine, now furiously scribbling a model petition for Monroe to copy, the situation had gone too far for tact. It was up to the government of the United States to force the issue through its minister. They owed him that. Under the influence of feelings he could not restrain, he produced a document which might serve as a model of everything that a diplomatic paper ought not to be.

Monroe had both the good sense to disregard it and the good nature not to hold it against Paine. He wrote instead an excellent letter which had the effect desired. On November 4, after an imprisonment of ten months, Paine was released. Monroe invited him to stay in his own house for as long as his illness or the state of his finances required it. A year later, Paine was still his guest, and Monroe hoped he would remain so until his death or his departure for America.

The kindness of Monroe is a pleasant episode, especially because Paine at this point in his life was at his most trying. Resentment of injustice had always been a dominant characteristic, and it now swallowed up his better instincts. For his actual imprisonment he blamed Robespierre, now dead; but what of America's neglect in the matter? Gouverneur Morris he ignored as a mere instrument of American policy. But what of Jefferson, Secretary of State, who might have insisted that Gouverneur Morris take steps? More important still, what of Washington, who had once given Paine his second coat, who had invited him to stay and pressed his merits on Congress? If there was any one person who might be expected to value Paine's services in the Revolution, it surely was Washington. Paine had constantly upheld him, had inspirited his army, and had been responsible for important efforts to keep his forces supplied. Surely he had a right to expect that Washington would have insisted on his release.

Feelings such as these were made more bitter by ill health. Despite the abcess in Paine's side which had developed in prison, he was able for a while to go about and even to some extent to take part in public affairs. In December, for instance, he was restored to the Convention; and there was some idle talk of compensating him with a pension. At last the Convention was turning once more to its original task, namely, the shaping of a constitution for the French Republic; but there was no question now of putting Paine on the committee. To those who had survived the Terror, he seemed a man of a past generation, though he was only in his middle fifties. The men whose finer feelings had expressed themselves in noble sentiments were dead; and though all admitted Paine was honest and virtuous, they thought him impractical. On July 7, 1795, he was permitted to stand once more on the Tribunal while someone read the translation of his speech; but the cause he was defending, universal suffrage, was one which only two members of the Convention had ever supported. When he said that the equality of man demanded it and that this principle was the life and soul of the Revolution, all listened with indifference. The new constitution, drawn up with little regard for such abstractions, was soon put into effect. The Convention dissolved, and Paine was left without an office.

While these events were taking place, Paine's health grew worse, not better. By September, 1795, he was confined to bed with a paralysis which prevented him from using his hands, so that he had to be fed and washed. The open wound in his side, the cause of this trouble, was agonizing to him. The rib was actually decaying, and he was not expected to live long.

Nothing could exceed the kindness of the Monroes. Mrs. Monroe found a devoted nurse, and eventually Paine's constitution triumphed. Illness, however, had increased the bitterness which imprisonment had fostered. Indeed, it is difficult not to believe that the poison in his body had gone to his head. *The Age of Reason* had by now drawn a number of replies from pious divines, who had noted that Paine's biblical scholarship was not profound. Actually he had written the treatise without a Bible to refer to, since an English Bible seemed unobtainable in France. He had now acquired one; and he wrote a second part to *The Age of Reason,* largely consisting of a venomous and detailed attack on the Holy Book. To those who admired him, it offered no positive doctrine, while those who hated him were not reconciled by chapter and verse. By publishing it, he merely did more damage to his reputation without pleasing anyone.

Even *The Age of Reason* took second place at this moment in Paine's life to more personal grievances. It is fair to say, however, that the course of American politics at the moment was also calculated to embitter his feelings. The John Jay treaty which Washington's government signed with England at this time represented an effort to clear away misunderstandings. Its actual terms, however, very favorable to England, were condemned even by many who saw an advantage in better relations between the two countries. To Paine, England's enemy, the treaty was a shameful betrayal of the spirit of the Revolution, which England had opposed in America and France.

Soon after his release, Paine had written a stiff letter to Washington, protesting the silence of the American government about his imprisonment, Morris' neglect of American interests in Paris, and the ignominious John Jay treaty. Luckily, he had shown this to Monroe, who had persuaded him not to send it. His bitterness, however, demanded expression. He sent off a manifesto against the John Jay treaty to be published in England. Monroe was critical of this treaty, too; but as a government official, he was embarrassed by a pamphlet written in his own house and condemning his government's policy. Hastily he wrote to Rufus King, American minister to Great Britain, begging him to use his influence to suppress it.

This episode was especially hard on Monroe because he had already asked Paine not to cause him difficulties by writing on American affairs while under his roof. Paine did not see the point of this. His own opinions were perfectly consistent, and there could be no question of his having been influenced by Monroe. Only grudgingly and as a favor to his host would he consent. Shortly, however, he forgot or ceased to care about this agreement. Monroe was soon embroiled in another affair, the result of a tactless letter Paine had sent off to Philadelphia for publication.

Even worse from Monroe's point of view was Paine's personal rancor against Washington, which continued to fester. During his illness it broke all bounds, and he actually sent Washington a letter accusing him of consenting to his imprisonment. He had come to the conclusion that there were only three possible motives for his country's neglect. Either Washington and the Federalists wanted to silence Paine so that they could turn American opinion against the French Revolution; or they feared Paine's opposition to their attempt to dominate America; or they wanted to please the British government for the sake of the John Jay treaty. With such suspicions in his head, Paine could not restrain his language, even though his conscience pricked him a little. "I ought not to have suspected you of treachery," he admitted, adding immediately, "I shall continue to think you treacherous until you give me cause to think otherwise."

Naturally enough, Paine received no answer to this epistle. Washington was a man of far too much dignity to defend himself against this sort of accusation. Most probably his inaction had been due to the advice of Gouverneur Morris that it would be dangerous to interfere. It is possible, however, that his Secretary of State had simply not told him about Paine's plight. If any blame in the matter is to be attached to Washington at all, it may be considered that he did not think it wise for America to come into conflict with the current leaders of the French Revolution.

What is more to the point, however, is that Paine and Washington, who had once agreed, now widely differed. Anxious to re-establish friendly relations with England, Washington had not been at all pleased at the dedication of *The Rights of Man* to himself. His letter acknowledging the fact had been slow to arrive and had been politely cold. *The Age of Reason* had greatly offended him. Paine, whose own opinions were, he felt, unchanged, was never able to see that Washington's were equally constant. Two very different men had been united by a war which was now over. It is a conspicuous difference between the two revolutions that the wars of the French one came to France late, so that faction was already flourishing by the time that they broke out. In America, on the other hand, the war of the Revolution temporarily united men who only gradually realized their differences. Indeed we may even say that *Common Sense* had produced a union of widely different characters. Thus Paine's friends in France were of his own party, whereas those in America were proving to be of many shades of opinion.

To be ignored infuriated Paine beyond bearing. He was now convinced that Washington had deliberately left him to die. He had the grace to move away from Monroe's house, but he paid no attention to the minister's entreaties that he should drop the subject. He composed a public letter which he sent to Benjamin Franklin Bache, Franklin's grandson and an intemperate enemy of Washington. Bache hastened to publish it, and an outcry resulted.

Paine described, of course, his imprisonment in detail, accusing Washington of refusing to claim him as an American. From there he went on to say it was common knowledge that Washington was incapable of friendship. So cold was he that he could "serve or desert a man, or a cause, with constitutional indifference." His only quality was a cool prudence which easily became hypocrisy. Even his generalship, so celebrated in the Revolution, had consisted in doing nothing while other people won great victories. As for his present administration, it was tyrannical, corrupt, and inefficient.

This indiscriminate blast was everywhere resented. Even those in opposition to Washington's policies were indignant about the mud thrown at the head of the state, the Father of his country. Paine's popularity, already undermined by *The Age of Reason,* was shattered in America, where it had always been strongest. He was even suspected of being in the pay of the French Convention.

Despite these vagaries, Paine had much to offer Monroe in the way of political advice. His detailed knowledge of personalities and politics was bound to be useful, so that at his best he began to re-establish the relationship he had held when Jefferson was minister in Paris. This was destroyed by Monroe's sudden recall, which signified a change in American policy to France. American diplomacy had little use for Paine as long as the interest of the Federalist government centered on England.

1797-1802
Last Years in France

Paine did not return to America after his release from prison, or even when his health was restored a year later. In his usual fashion, he planned to do so, changed his mind, then changed it again. In March, 1797, when Monroe left France, Paine actually got as far as Le Havre to wait for a suitable vessel going to the United States. Only after several months did he decide he dared not risk it, lest the British seize him on the high seas as a traitor. Perhaps he was wise, for he later heard that the vessel on which Monroe had sailed was stopped by a British frigate which searched it from end to end for Thomas Paine. The remarkable thing is that Paine should even have considered sailing if the British were really so eager to get him in their power.

There were other reasons for delaying his departure which may have influenced him as strongly. What was he to do in America? After insulting the head of the government, he could hardly hope his expert knowledge of French affairs would be officially used. He might have devoted himself to anti-Federalist propaganda; but even Paine, who was always optimistic, must have known that his prestige was at a low ebb.

Meanwhile, in France he sought opportunities to serve the cause of the Revolution. French opinion had been as much outraged by the John Jay treaty as Paine's own. As the French saw the matter, the United States had broken the alliance signed with France in 1778 by agreeing that the British might confiscate enemy property shipped on neutral vessels. The French government had made its objections known to Monroe as soon as the treaty terms were made public; and it had hoped that the President and Congress would not ratify them. When they did so, the French indignantly recalled their minister from the United States; and when Charles Pinckney arrived in Paris to replace Monroe, the Minister of Foreign Affairs would not receive him. Meanwhile, in active retaliation, the French seized American ships. In an effort at reconciliation, President Adams, in the spring of 1797, appointed Pinckney, Marshall, and Gerry as special envoys to discuss the whole subject with France.

By this time, Paine had his own idea about how to handle the maritime problem. He had drawn up a scheme by which neutral nations should publicly declare that the ports of all would be closed to any nation which molested any one of them. It is a notion typical of Paine, far-reaching, even lofty, but conceived in disregard of the facts, since America would hardly consent to a flat violation of the John Jay treaty so recently signed. This, after all, had allowed the British to search neutral ships. Paine sent an outline of his plan to Talleyrand, now French Foreign Minister, who was not unnaturally pleased with the advantage which it promised France in breaking the British blockade.

Marshall, who had just arrived in France to take up negotiations, next received a visit from a friend of Paine's who tried to persuade him that this was the wrong moment to ask for concessions. The Directors, who under the present constitution governed France, had a plan before them which would be advantageous to the United States. If, therefore, the American commissioners would have a little patience, affairs would soon go better.

That very night Paine sent Marshall a copy of this plan with a covering letter in which he gave a good deal of advice. The rumor was that the United States was ready to grant to France the maritime rights which had been given to England under the John Jay treaty. Paine warned Marshall that France already claimed these as a consequence of the treaty of 1778, and that therefore she would be insulted by such an offer. He thought also that it would be unwise to press for compensation for the seizure of American ships. France was deeply offended at American ingratitude; and it would not be easy to soothe her without some constructive proposal like his own, which went far beyond the original grievance.

Marshall received this unsought advice unwillingly, describing Paine's letter in his diary as "an insult which ought to be received with that coldness which would forbid the repetition of it." To his government he sent a report on the plan, remarking that from the support "this man" received, he could only imagine that the pamphlet was written with the knowledge and approval of the French government. Thus far had Paine's credit slipped with the representatives of the American people.

This rebuff does much to explain why Paine lingered in France, where his influence could be greater than in America. He was now living with Nicolas de Bonneville, a printer who had brought out the second half of *The Rights of Man* in French. Bonneville was devoted to the ideals of a revolutionary club called *Le Cercle Social,* which met for discussions on the nature of the ideal society. Alliance with him gave Paine an outlet and an audience, since Bonneville published a paper called *le Bien Informé* which had a wide influence.

Curiously enough, one of the uses which Paine made of this publication was to support a coup in September, 1797, overthrowing constitutional government in favor of a dictatorship by the Directory. There had been a conspiracy, however, to restore the monarchy, so that Paine was grateful for any strong government which would preserve the gains of the Revolution. Thus as the Directory gave place to Napoleon, Paine was swept along by the rising tide of French nationalism, by the need for leadership in war, and by fear of reaction. It was only as he saw dictatorship harden that he once more began to think of going home.

By 1797, the gains of the Revolution in France had nearly all been made. The revolutionary struggle had been transferred to the war, which was increasingly involving the total resources of Europe. Cut off from further share in constitution-making, Paine naturally turned his attention to war plans. Being English-speaking, he was familiar with the Irish republican rebels who circulated in Paris. But whereas their hopes were for an invasion of Ireland, financed and assisted by the French, Paine planned for an attack on England herself.

It would be easier, he pointed out in the *Bien Informé,* to land ten thousand men in England than send them to fight the British in India. Having now possession of the Dutch coast, France owned excellent harbors for the purpose; and ten million livres would construct a thousand gunboats. Unalterably convinced that French resources were far greater than those of England, Paine did not even think it necessary to call for increased taxes. Assuming the adult males of France to be around five million, of whom half were too poor to give anything, he assesses the rest on a descending scale for voluntary contributions from twelve livres to twenty sous. For his own part, poor though he was, he offered a hundred livres to the great project.

Paine had been working on plans for this invasion since 1796, when he had drawn up a document, complete with map, on the construction and operation of the navy that would be required. He pressed the whole upon the Directory which, according to him, actually ordered the construction of two hundred and fifty boats. When the project was taken up by Napoleon in 1800, Paine naturally came into prominence. A romantic anecdote which may quite possibly have been derived from Paine's own account says that Napoleon invited him to dinner, told him that every city of the universe ought to put up a golden statue of him, and assured him that he slept with a copy of *The Rights of Man* under his pillow. More practically, he asked him to accompany the invasion force as a political adviser, which Paine was glad to do, still perfectly certain that the English people would rise when given a chance.

In the last years of the century, however, while this project still hung fire, Paine was ready to compromise in favor of an invasion of Ireland. We see him on St. Patrick's Day, 1798, sitting at a national banquet on the left of the Irish chieftain Napper-Tandy. In the summer of the same year he presented an Irish petition to the Directory, begging for a thousand men and five thousand guns, merely to ensure that those who wished to rise in Ireland would not be cut to pieces for want of a nucleus around which they might rally. Shortly after, he wrote to call the Directory's attention to the fate of Irish officers having commissions in the French service who, when captured, were hanged as traitors. Let Irish officers who served King George be considered hostages for the safety of their compatriots. A similar arrangement had saved the life of General Charles Lee during the American Revolution.

It is to Wolfe Tone, one of these Irish revolutionaries, that we owe the best description of Paine during these years. Tone liked him, praised his conversation, and remarked that his humor, which was often clumsy in print, became witty in speech. On the other hand, Paine was incredibly vain. Tone, who had known Burke in England, said that Burke had been completely shattered by the death of his only son Richard. Paine immediately retorted that it was *The Rights of Man* which had broken his heart. *"Paine has no children!"* wrote Tone indignantly.

Paine was still drinking heavily, as Tone remarked. Another visitor described his face as blotched and his hand as unsteady, though after he had been given a glass of brandy he talked well: "an acute reasoner, in fact, a monstrous clever man." Yet another speaks of him as well-dressed, gentlemanly, and fascinating to talk to.

Paine was usually tidy in person, and he looks conspicuously neat in all known portraits. On the other hand, he was in his sixties by now and had lived as a bachelor nearly all his life in cramped quarters. He was probably careless by nature and habit. One of his visitors, more fastidious than many, comments on the disorder of his room with its unswept hearth and general dirtiness. Its furnishings included three shelves of cardboard boxes which he used for filing papers, two trunks, and a dresser, which looked like an old piece of kitchen equipment and was covered with papers.

In a corner lay the bars of his model iron bridge. By now Bonneville's paper had been suppressed by the government, and Paine had lost his last chance of speaking out in France. He was turning back to science, painstakingly constructing two models of his bridge, a carpenter's plane, a carriage wheel, and a crane constructed on a new principle. His money was running low; and as usual with him, he was looking around for ways to make his fortune.

Probably his most intimate friend was Joel Barlow, Connecticut wit, revolutionist, and poet, who was like himself an honorary citizen of France. Barlow had kept aloof from the French political struggle and had accumulated a fair fortune, mainly by running contraband goods across war frontiers. Like Paine, he dabbled in science. Both, therefore, were interested when a fellow American turned up in Paris to market an invention which he claimed would put an end to naval war. This was Robert Fulton, who had improved and adapted a primitive submarine which had failed to be effective against the British fleet in 1776.

Since France was inferior to England on the sea, the destruction of navies had an instant and natural appeal in Paris. It is true that Fulton wanted prize money on a very liberal scale and that the Directors, hard-headed though they were, seemed shocked at his weapon. Delays enabled Fulton to make improvements; and he was clever enough to let the British get wind of his idea, so that presently a question about his submarine asked in the House of Lords underlined his importance.

Fulton had previously spent some years in England and had done work there on designing canals. Thus it is not surprising to find that in 1800 Paine produced a paper on the development of French resources with special attention to canals and iron bridges. Meanwhile, Fulton's personal attractions won the heart of Joel Barlow, who treated him like a son.

The Directory was unable to make up its mind about Fulton; but when Napoleon was put in command of the Army of England, he was not so hesitant. Thus at the very moment when Paine was agreeing to become Napoleon's adviser, Fulton's submarine was having a trial in Brest harbor, where it blew up a small boat placed for the purpose. On the twelfth of September, 1800, Fulton ventured out to sea with the object of altering history by blowing up a British squadron. But the tide changed before he was in position, and he had to stay submerged for six hours in great discomfort. When at last he surfaced again, the sea was empty. The British secret service had warned their ships, which had hastily departed.

This adventure of Fulton's proved that he had daring. His fine pretensions of being a benefactor to mankind were less convincing, since in 1802 he was again in England, offering to sell his invention there. But Fulton's abilities were certainly great. Soon he became interested in designs for a steamboat. Paine himself had discussed such a project with several people, including Fitch, who had by now produced one boat. But Fitch, mechanic rather than engineer, had by no means solved all the problems of design and was not able to explain how future boats were to be constructed. This Fulton now prepared to do, having found himself a wealthy patron in Robert Livingston, American minister to France, who had for some time been interested in steamboat construction.

While this connection drew Paine's thoughts back to engineering, his political influence had disappeared. Both he and Bonneville were too outspoken to please the Directory, which actually suspected Paine of intrigue with British agents. The *Bien Informé* was first suspended for publishing a jest about one of the Directors. Paine was successful in getting this ban lifted, but some time later Bonneville compared Napoleon to Cromwell, the English dictator, and was sent to prison for the offence. The offices of the *Bien Informé* were finally closed.

Clearly it was little use commenting on political matters if censorship was to be so strict. In 1799, Paine went away to spend a winter with one of the Belgian friends who had nursed him in prison. While he was there, he went up to spend a few days in Holland with a general of French troops who were being attacked by the British. He was in high hopes of seeing the last of John Bull, as he said; but it was the French who were defeated. He went back to Paris, only to be informed through the Minister of Police that his behavior was suspect, and that he would be deported to America at the very next complaint received against him.

From this time Paine refrained from political writing, yet neither his character nor the friends whom he knew best were made for caution. Barlow, for instance, did not scruple to describe Napoleon as "the Butcher of Liberty" at a dinner which Fulton, Paine, and a member of the

French Senate attended. As for Paine himself, he grew more melancholy with disappointment over the course of the Revolution. His admiration for Napoleon had not lasted long, and he thought that America was now the world's only genuine republic. In one of his waves of optimism he calculated that he was worth about seven thousand pounds if he could get back to that country. The estate which had been granted him in New York produced little income; and the house which stood on it had burned down. Paine was coming, in fact, to the end of his resources in France; and the only wonder is that they had lasted so long. In fact, it was time he went home to earn money.

1802-09
Last Years in America

Paine's most constant friend in America during the years of his absence had been Thomas Jefferson. During the early days of the French Revolution, when Jefferson was minister in Paris and in the confidence of Lafayette, they had found that their beliefs had much in common. When Paine had published *The Rights of Man* in 1791, Jefferson had borrowed the only copy in America on the condition that he should forward it when he had finished to a publisher who was to bring out an American edition. This he duly did, accompanying it by a letter expressing pleasure that something was being said to counter the political heresies which were springing up in the country.

Jefferson was Secretary of State at the time, and the publisher boosted sales by printing his incautious statement in the front of the book. Everyone who read it perceived that the political heresy referred to was Federalism, and that Jefferson saw *The Rights of Man* as an answer to Adams' *Discourses on Davila*. In other words, the Secretary of State was endorsing Paine's pamphlet as an attack upon the Vice-President. A tremendous uproar resulted; and when Jefferson tried to calm feelings by explaining he had not intended the letter to be published, he merely offended his friends without placating his enemies. Moreover the British, preparing to prosecute the author of the *Rights* were offended at its being dedicated to the American President and endorsed by his Secretary of State.

This episode helped to harden party lines in America, identifying the Republican party with support of the French Revolution, while the Federalists leaned towards its enemy, England. Jefferson, though personally the kindliest of men, was almost pleased with the execution of Louis XVI because he thought it would serve as an awful warning to Federalists who wanted a king in America. He understood the idealism which had led Paine to take his seat in the Convention, sympathized with Paine's sufferings under the Terror, and was eager to hope that France had now purged herself.

The Age of Reason proved no shock to Jefferson, partly because he shared many of its beliefs, and partly because the outcry in the Federalist press annoyed him. Adams himself was a Unitarian, and did not believe in the Trinity, so that Jefferson thought it was the sheerest hypocrisy for Federalists to denounce Paine for denying the divinity of Christ. Besides, Paine's opinions, though tactlessly expressed, were based on information available to all educated men.

The letter to Washington was certainly imprudent; but Paine's hatred of the John Jay treaty was no greater than Jefferson's own. Both were alarmed at the antidemocratic tendencies of Washington's government. Thus, different though they were in their modes of expression, they represented the same point of view. While Marshall in France coldly rejected Paine's proposal for an alliance of neutral nations, Thomas Jefferson arranged to publish his plan in America.

In 1801, at the very time when Paine was being threatened by the suspicions of the Directory, Thomas Jefferson became President of the United States. Thus precisely at the moment when Paine saw he was useless in Europe, he had a chance to put his expert knowledge at the disposal of the President. Everything pointed to the wisdom of going home: his financial difficulties, his increasing dislike of dictatorship, and the final suppression of the *Bien Informé*. Unless the French invasion of England should come to pass, which was beginning to seem less likely, Paine could be more influential in America.

This was all very true, but how was he to cross the Atlantic? If the British had wanted to catch him in 1797, they were far more eager in 1800, when he was Napoleon's official adviser for the invasion of England. The British blockade had tightened up, and their spies were everywhere. Paine wrote to Jefferson that he dared not put to sea except in a warship.

Jefferson was sympathetic, and it happened that he was sending the *Maryland* to France in the spring of 1801 to carry over the draft of a new treaty which was to be ratified in Paris. Accordingly, he wrote to Paine that the *Maryland* had instructions to take him abroad if he could leave at such short notice. Unfortunately Paine began to boast of receiving a letter in which the President had personally invited him to return aboard a naval vessel. A notice appeared in the French press, implying that Jefferson's invitation had been unsolicited and that a warship was being despatched to France expressly to fetch Paine.

The Federalist press raised an extraordinary uproar. It is to be remembered that Jefferson was deliberately destroying the image of the Presidency which his predecessors had established. Those who dropped in to see him in the informal fashion of those days were apt to find him in a worn brown coat and corduroy breeches, together with old knitted stockings economically re-footed with wool of a different color. In fact, he was deliberately shabby, and he affected a red waistcoat which made people say he looked like a Jacobin. Jefferson was posing as a man of the people rather than the conventional head of a state. He was demonstrating what he thought the president of a republic should be to a world in which heads of state were formal. His free-and-easy ways recalled French excesses.

Such being the spirit of Jefferson's presidency, the Federalists hastened to quote violent passages from *The Age of Reason* and to assert that the President had personally summoned their notorious author to Washington. The Jeffersonians found it necessary to print a semi-apology, explaining that Paine had asked for passage before the election and that the warship had been going in any case. Surely it was possible for Jefferson to show charity towards Paine in misfortune without sharing his religious convictions. Surely also the country might be grateful for Paine's past services, even if he now admitted to opinions which were disliked.

This paragraph, sent to Paine by a well-wisher, offended him deeply by its reference to charity. He was quick to suppose that Jefferson was preparing to deny his friendship. In any case, it was not convenient to leave with the *Maryland,* perhaps because the invasion of England still hung in the air. Another American warship was bound to visit France before long to bring over Livingston, who was to be the new American minister, Paine delayed; but when Livingston did arrive, the vessel which brought him went on to the Mediterranean instead of going home.

By 1802, the situation was altered by a pause in the long war between France and England. Napoleon, needing a breathing-space, made peace on advantageous terms. The seas were opened for Paine to leave at any time he pleased.

He did not part from his friends without regret. Indeed, he urged the Bonnevilles to follow as soon as he had re-established his position in the only land of freedom. Thomas Rickman, his old friend from Lewes, who had by now taken refuge in France from government persecution, went down to Havre with him to see him off and wrote an emotional, if not especially poetic stanza of farewell.

He landed at Baltimore and was given a public welcome by noisy Republicans. Federalists, on the other hand, were delighted to have him arrested for debt a few days later at the instance of a man who had lent him fifty guineas when he was in the Luxembourg. Paine did not deny the fact, but stated that the claimant had merely been the agent for another, to whom alone he was prepared to pay the money. The matter was soon settled, but the incident left an unpleasantness which must have been heightened by the lurid stories appearing in Federalist papers about Paine's character, his habits, his opinions, and the way in which every right-minded person disliked him.

It did not take him long to discover that former intimates, even including Benjamin Rush, thought *The Age of Reason* sufficient pretext for breaking off their friendship. He had forwarded to Thomas Jefferson cases containing models of his iron bridge, his new carriage wheel, and the rest of his inventions. Instead of hastening to discuss these plans, Jefferson put him off on the grounds that he was busy. Immediately Paine was offended and accused Jefferson of finding it politically embarrassing to see him.

Jefferson replied that he had always insisted it was a duty to show respect to Paine for his past services. He did not fear what the Federalists could say. Paine dined with him and was seen in his company by some of those indignant visitors who sneered at the President's clothes. The Vice-President invited Paine out, too, as did the Secretaries of the Treasury and War. Congress, however, was cold; and a general feeling existed that it was unwise to know Paine. Most of his evenings were spent in the public rooms of Lovell's Hotel, where those who would not speak with him pressed in to stare.

Used to political rebuffs by now, Paine began immediately to publish a series of letters "To the Citizens of the United States." Since the first two were anti-Federalist in tone and offered a defense of Paine's political views, they were well received by the Republican press. Unfortunately, the third was Paine's answer to Federalist attacks on his religion. Paine was anxious to show that Providence was on his side; and he therefore related his escapes from the guillotine and from the British, dwelling heavily on the miraculous nature of each. At home, he avowed, his property had increased in value; his health was good; and his mind was tranquil. Such signs of divine favor were positive evidence that his religious views could not be blasphemous.

It was not the tone of this peculiar letter, but its subject which annoyed Paine's supporters. In their view, the less he said about religion the better, for they did not sympathize with his conviction that all his opinions hung together. It is notable that, about a year later, when Paine was visiting in Connecticut, a group of Republicans from New London went to see him. One of these, though personally friendly to Paine, was appalled to discover that he was planning a third part to *The Age of Reason*. It had been possible, he felt, to defend the original pamphlet on the grounds that it had been written as an attack on atheism in France. The mere thought of another part, presumably attacking Puritanism in New England and Christianity throughout the United States, affected him with such horror that he wrote imploring Jefferson to stop the publication.

With Paine in such a mood, it was not easy for Jefferson to make use of his experience. He did, indeed, ask his opinion on French matters, notably on what to do about Louisiana, concealing from him that he had already made up his mind to purchase it. Paine entirely agreed with his policy and helpfully published a letter in May, 1803, pointing out that Federalist impatience could only bring on disaster. If the United States seized New Orleans by force, it would be blockaded by a French fleet and commercially ruined. To Monroe, who was setting off for France to negotiate the purchase, he gave introductory letters and a memorandum, explaining how to approach the present politicians and telling him which was the only man who knew Louisiana.

His interest did not end here, and after the purchase he was ready with advice on how to reconcile the Senate and what sort of government to plan for the territory. He even went so far as to tell Jefferson that he had thousands of English admirers whom he might persuade to flee from tyranny and settle in the new lands.

It is easy to see that this sort of well-meant assistance was part useful and part not. Jefferson was courteous with thanks but did not offer the official post which was what Paine really wanted. Paine was past his middle sixties, and the drawbacks which had hung about him all his life were greater than ever. In an age when politics were in the hands of an educated class, Paine had never quite the manners of a gentleman. He had always drunk a good deal; and his enemies circulated unpleasant stories about his personal habits. Most of these are too nasty to be believed, but his friends in rushing to his defense may have had a tendency to exaggerate his virtues. Paine may not have been dirty and drunken, but he was probably capable of drinking enough to become unreasonable or quarrelsome in argument. In these last years of his life his nose, which was always prominent, became swollen and inflamed. His friends put the condition down to skin disease, his enemies to drink. There seems no doubt at least that the affliction gave him a disreputable appearance.

He was no more discreet than he had ever been. His Republican visitors in Connecticut found his conversation pleasant until he had "made free with ardent spirits." In this condition he read aloud to them a private letter from Jefferson thanking him for his advice about Louisiana. It was an additional drawback as politics then were that Paine was unable to adapt to passing changes. Politicians might talk of ways and means, might make concessions to expediency. Paine's principles were part of a whole which never could be altered.

If a job and a salary were not forthcoming, Paine could not linger in Washington. He depended entirely on the property which he had left, chiefly consisting of the house in Bordentown and the farm in New Rochelle which had been given to him by the State of New York. It was time that he went to inspect them both and make plans for the future.

It was sad to find how many old friends, such as Dr. Benjamin Rush, were ready to turn their backs on the author of *The Age of Reason*. Colonel Kirkbride of Bordentown was not one of these. Indeed, his admiration for Paine was increased by the years which had gone past. Unfortunately, however, neither the Colonel nor his friend were popular in the countryside. When they tried to take a stagecoach from Trenton to New York, the proprietor said he would be damned if an infidel like Tom Paine should ride in his stage. His rival, equally emphatic, declared that his stage had been struck by lightning once and that he did not propose to risk divine displeasure again. Paine and Kirkbride were forced to hire a chaise, which was held up by a mob coming to meet them with a drummer beating the rogue's march. The two drove boldly through; and people scattered, though they tried to frighten the horses by drumming and hallooing.

New York was less unfriendly because it was large enough to have a Republican club, which gave Paine a dinner. Besides this, there was a Deistical Society there which shared Paine's religious beliefs. It was founded and held together by a certain Elihu Palmer, who had unfortunately been blinded by an attack of yellow fever during a Philadelphia epidemic. Despite this sign of divine ill favor, he had gathered together a little group in New

York and was planning to erect there a Temple of Nature. Meanwhile, about the time of Paine's arrival Palmer established a deistical paper called *The Prospect, or View of the Moral World*.

To this small religious sect, Paine was a tremendous boon. They hoped to use his matchless powers of propaganda in *The Prospect*. They looked on him personally as a very great man and pressed him to stay among them. For two months he did so until an epidemic of yellow fever made it more prudent to go on a round of visits. All the same, he was not quite convinced that his future lay with the group. No doubt about it, they were a small, odd sect, completely obscure and only too likely to remain so. He was happy to write for *The Prospect,* but he was looking for a larger audience.

For a while he thought of going back to France, in case Napoleon's invasion of England should be successful. It would indeed have been the crown of his career if he had been able to draw up a new constitution for England. The British consul-general in New York warned his superiors that Paine might put to sea and should be arrested. As usual, however, Paine was incapable of prompt decision. Napoleon's attention was diverted by troubles in Europe, and in 1805 the battle of Trafalgar put an end to every chance of a naval venture against Britain.

Meanwhile, Paine had been forced to consider once more the question of finances. Neither the bridge nor the other inventions had produced a penny, and it soon became fairly clear they would never do so. His estate in New Rochelle needed managing if he was to live on its income, and he suddenly found himself with private obligations.

Times were bad in France for honest republican visionaries like Bonneville. He had promised Paine to try his fortune in the United States, but the authorities preferred to keep him under their eye. However, they raised no objection to the departure of Mme. Bonneville and her three sons to take advantage of the offers which Paine had made to them. Thus in 1803, Paine suddenly found himself with four dependents.

He rose nobly to the occasion, writing to Bonneville that he would see that the family wanted for nothing and would leave them his estate when he died. For the present he could not house them in New Rochelle because, his house having burned down, he was engaged in expanding a small cottage on the place for his own residence. He established the Bonnevilles in Bordentown, while he lived partly in New York and partly in New Rochelle, boarding in the village.

This arrangement was not practicable for long. Mme. Bonneville, an energetic Parisian woman in her mid-thirties, was bored beyond endurance by the sleepiness of a small American town which was not even close to the center of the government. She insisted on coming to New York, where Paine tried to set her up in business as a French teacher, with only fair success.

All in all, Mme. Bonneville became a real problem. She was not a practical woman or a good manager on a small income. Her oldest son disliked America and soon returned to France. Paine took a special interest in the second one, Thomas Paine Bonneville; but he was determined to be fair. Mme. Bonneville was willing to let him send young Thomas to a tutor, but she was determined to keep at least Benjamin, her youngest, with her. Paine insisted that he would not give an education to one without the other. The dispute ended by the lady and both her sons being established in New Rochelle, where Paine at last had made his cottage habitable.

This arrangement, too, failed to solve the problem. Mme. Bonneville found New Rochelle no better than Bordentown. Nor was she in the least practical. As Paine said angrily, she would not so much as make an apple dumpling for her children. Eventually she found employment in New York as a governess and was able to have Benjamin with her.

Thomas remained in New Rochelle with Paine, who took his responsibility seriously and sent the boy to school. Their situation, however, was not comfortable. Most of the villagers thought Paine had sold himself to the devil and used him as a bogeyman to frighten naughty children. One of these later recalled going with two or three other boys to steal apples from Paine's orchard. To their dismay he saw them; but instead of pouncing on them, he came out and helped them to get the best, patting them on the head and talking cheerfully.

This pleasant incident is not uncharacteristic of the Paine who wrote so kindly to a young girl on her marriage, who took such trouble over the Bonnevilles, who forgave a widow two years' rent, and who, according to his friends, produced from his pockets nuts and other trifles for small boys. All the same, he was a lonely man and one not easy to understand.

The farm contained about a hundred cultivated acres, plus an equal amount of grazing land and of timber. Paine was able to sell a fifth for about four thousand dollars and to paper two bedrooms in his cottage for himself and the Bonnevilles. In his usual bachelor fashion, however, his furnishings were casual. He had six chairs and a table, a straw bed, a featherbed, and a bag of straw for Thomas. In addition he had a number of cooking utensils and says he lived on fruit pies, dumplings, milk, and tea, with meat when he could get it. He returned to New York from time to time, to visit his deistical friends, but was careful to board Thomas with one of his acquaintances in the village.

The farm had originally been cared for on Paine's behalf by a man named Christopher Derrick. Presently Paine discharged him and turned him off the farm to live in the village. For a while, however, he still came to work off a debt of $48 he owed Paine. Apparently this arrangement was a grievance, because on Christmas Eve of 1805 he started drinking, borrowed a gun, and discharged it at Paine, who was sitting in the living room of his cottage on one of his six chairs. The bullet went through the wall just underneath the window, but missed Paine. The incident, however, was reported everywhere, including France and England, as an example of how greatly he was hated.

One might suppose such notoriety would have helped him to gain influence again, but Paine was out of date. He had lost his position in American politics by his absence of twenty years. Yet even had he remained and understood better its personalities and problems, it is impossible to suppose that he would have retained his old reputation. Paine was essentially a man of first principles and great causes. When politics became a question of party, small issues arising from day to day took precedence over large ones. It is true there were principles behind the struggle between Republican and Federalist. But these were expressed in practical detail and very often worked out in compromises. Paine, though fertile in suggestions, was no better than a thousand others on a practical level. For compromise he had never had any talent.

He did not hesitate to express his opinions, but the age of revolution had exhausted itself in America. There was nothing worthy of Paine's peculiar powers to be said in attacking either Federalists in general or certain particular ones. His suggestions for fortifying the port of New York were not taken seriously. Far more heat was engendered by the unkind rumor that a scheme for a French invasion of the United States which Bonneville had published in the *Bien Informé* some years ago had been written by Paine.

He was not silenced by neglect because it was in his nature to comment on political events, but even vanity could not deceive him into thinking that his prospects were good. Nearing seventy, he was growing steadily poorer, while still responsible for three dependents. The remembrance of the extreme old age of his mother returned to worry him. He had no son to keep him from destitution.

Once more he thought of an edition of his works; but if subscriptions had not come in after the Revolution, they were hardly likely to do so many years later. Desperately he wondered if Jefferson could induce the Virginia legislature to award him a tract of land, though the motion to do so had been defeated in 1784. He wrote to him on the subject; and Jefferson, puzzled perhaps about what to say, did not immediately answer. Paine's feelings were growing too sensitive, and he dashed off an angry note in the third person: "Thomas Paine's compliments to Mr. Jefferson desires to be informed if he received a letter

from him . . ." Impulsively he sent it without even reading it through to see if it made sense.

Tactfully Jefferson replied that he had put off his answer because nothing could be done until the meetings of
Congress and the Virginia legislature. Meanwhile he did
his best by sending Paine's letter to a Virginia friend and
asking him to sound out the legislators. Nothing came of
this, and an application by Paine to the Vice-President
brought no result.

If the old claim could not be revived, perhaps he might
still be rewarded by an official position. In 1806, Napoleon mastered Europe in the battle of Austerlitz, which
caused the dying Pitt to say to his attendants, "Roll up
that map. It will not be wanted again these ten years."
While this situation was developing, Paine had offered
himself as a special envoy to negotiate with Napoleon.
Jefferson had put him off, explaining that for the moment
there were people on the spot to handle all business.

It was hard to grow unimportant, poor, and old; but
worse was to follow. In New Rochelle that very same year
election inspectors refused Paine the right to vote on the
ground that he was not an American citizen. Gouverneur
Morris, they said, had not reclaimed him from prison in
France, and Washington had "refused to do it." In such
fashion did Paine's own heated accusations of Washington
come home to roost.

Nothing could have been more unkind than that his
citizenship, so precious for so long, should have been denied him in that very township where New York had rewarded him with an estate. It stung him into a frenzy of
action; and he wrote Barlow, Madison, Monroe, Clinton,

and others for documents bearing on his case. According to Mme. Bonneville, who should have known, he carried the case to court before he died—and lost it. No record, however, can be traced of the trial or its verdict.

He can hardly have wished to remain in New Rochelle, where apparently he was sunk in depression. Elihu Palmer was dead, but the group in New York had not forgotten Paine. Among them was a blacksmith and veterinarian named William Carver, who had been a boy in Lewes long ago and had occasionally saddled Paine's horse. Carver had never acquired much education, but he was intelligent and a follower of Paine in politics as well as religion. He had prospered in New York, and Paine had stayed with him on several occasions when he visited the deists. Carver now rode out from New York and, finding Paine perhaps at the end of a drunken debauch, but certainly unwell, depressed, and far from his usual self, strongly urged him to leave New Rochelle for good. He, Carver, would give him a permanent room in his house, where he would be among his real friends.

Paine was happy to accept, but the arrangement did not turn out well. Some ten weeks later, as he was going upstairs at Carver's after a frugal supper of bread and butter, he suffered a stroke and fell downstairs, injuring himself so badly that he had to be lifted in and out of bed for several weeks. Elihu Palmer's widow, who lived on the same street, was hired to nurse him; and with her aid he eventually recovered sufficiently to seek another lodging.

At this point Carver demanded $150 to pay Paine's board and that of Mrs. Palmer. Paine, who apparently had made no financial agreement, was highly indignant. Both parties exaggerated their wrongs. Carver and his wife, Paine said, had never been civil. His tea and coffee were given him last and were often not fit to drink. He had to provide his own bedding. His room had been only a closet off the front room, while Mrs. Palmer had neither a room of her own nor access to a fire. Finally, Carver had left him alone on the night that he was stricken.

Carver retorted with a fearsome account of Paine's disgusting condition in New Rochelle, unshaved for a couple of weeks, his shirt in rags, filthy and evil-smelling, his nails like bird's claws. He added a hint that Mme. Bonneville was Paine's mistress and her boys were his own. This correspondence he later turned over to a man named Cheetham, who published a slanderous biography of Paine. Mme. Bonneville sued him for his insinuations and won her case; but Cheetham was given a nominal fine and actually commended for having defended the cause of religion.

Luckily for Paine, he found hospitality with John Wesley Jarvis, the American portrait painter, who was at this time in his thirties. Jarvis, a bachelor and something of a Bohemian, liked to talk and was a celebrated wit. He took to Paine and used to argue with him on religion, the rights of man, and all the causes to which the elder man had devoted his life. Far from finding him drunken, dirty, or unpleasant, Jarvis described him as one of the most pleasant companions he had met with, "for an old man."

It was while he was staying with Jarvis that Paine published an "Essay on Dream," which examines passages in the Bible where doctrine is based on dreams. He spoke to Jarvis about this, inquiring what the reviewers had said.

Jarvis replied that he had not seen any comment. His enemies were cunning, said Paine defiantly. They knew that if they abused his work, people would read it.

Jarvis retorted that if Paine wanted to publish a popular book, he should write his recantation. "You know the time must soon come when, like Voltaire and others, you will recant all you have said on the subject of religion." Surely it would be wiser, Jarvis pointed out, to do this while he could still enjoy the profits, rather than waiting till his deathbed.

"I do not know," replied Paine, "what I may do when infested by disease and pain; I may become a second child; and designing people may entrap me into saying anything; or they may put into my mouth what I never said." Therefore while he was in perfect health, he repeated to Jarvis the opinions he had expressed in *The Age of Reason*.

He had never ceased to like his nap after dinner; and while he was sleeping one day, a very old lady in a scarlet cloak persuaded Jarvis that she really had to see him. She was taken into his bedroom and solemnly told him: "I come from Almighty God to tell you that if you do not repent of your sins and believe in our blessed Saviour Jesus Christ, you will be damned."

"Pooh, pooh, it is not true," said Paine, rising on one elbow. "You were not sent with any such impertinent message. Jarvis, make her go away. Pshaw, he would not send such a foolish ugly old woman as you about with his messages. Go away. Go back—shut the door!"

The old lady retired, raising both her hands in astonished horror.

This story is only one of several. Well-meaning people who heard that Paine was in failing health persuaded themselves that they might win a triumph for God by playing on what they supposed was his fear of hell. They were mistaken. Paine liked dying no better than the next man, but his conscience was clear. In any case, his end was not yet very close. He was still able to enjoy old friends and make new enemies.

It was at this time, the last pleasant period of his life, that he again met Robert Fulton. When Napoleon lost interest in his submarine, Fulton had turned his attention to steamboat construction, finding in Livingston, the minister to Paris, a patron with some experience in the project and plenty of money. This sent Fulton to England, where all the best steam engines were made, to buy one. Perhaps he did not explain to Paine that, while he had been there, he had offered to sell his submarine to the British for a hundred thousand pounds with something very much like blackmail in mind. To Napoleon he had talked of doing humanity a favor by putting an end to naval war. To the British he pointed out that by suppressing his invention they could continue to fight Napoleon with the weapon of naval blockade. Nothing had come of his ingenious schemes because the battle of Trafalgar had destroyed all chance of Napoleon's challenging the British on the sea. Even the submarine could not now reverse the situation; and the British could afford to ignore Fulton, which forced him back on his scheme of designing a steamboat.

He was in America now, building his boat on the Hudson with Livingston's money to bear the expense. His maneuvers to make money out of the submarine make it abundantly clear that Fulton was not really a man of principle, as Paine was. All the same, he was a liberal by choice, a good talker, and an outstandingly pleasant man.

He was the protégé of Paine's friend Joel Barlow, and he
was involved in exactly the kind of project to interest
Paine. Fulton's steamboat was not original, not even the
first of its kind; but it was the first steamboat in which the
mechanical difficulties were really understood.

There was clearly life in Paine yet, and his quarrel with
James Cheetham during these last days in New York
bears witness to it. Cheetham, an Englishman and by
trade a hatter, had been a supporter of *The Rights of Man.*
In 1798, there had been riots in Manchester; and Cheetham had been charged with a conspiracy to overthrow the
government. He fled to the United States, where he soon
became the publisher of *The American Citizen,* the chief
Republican paper.

Very soon after Paine returned from France, Cheetham
made his acquaintance; and as soon as Paine was established in New York, he began to write regularly for *The
American Citizen.* In 1807, however, Cheetham began to
change the policy of his paper. About this time and probably for this reason he altered an article of Paine's before
publishing it. Paine, naturally indignant, broke with Cheetham and became a contributor to the *Public Advertiser.*

The next thing that happened was that the *Citizen* began to criticize what Paine was writing in the *Public Advertiser.* Paine leaped into print with a direct attack on
Cheetham of a sort more common then than now. "Mr.
Cheetham in his rage for attacking every body and every
thing that is not his own (for he is an ugly tempered man,
and he carries the evidence of it in the vulgarity and for-
bidingness of his countenance . . .) has attacked me on
the ground of my political works, and in doing this he
has exposed the barrenness of his political understanding."

A controversy started in this style was bound to flourish. Paine, resenting an attack by Cheetham on French militarism, described him as a "prejudiced and surly tempered John Bull" and called it impertinence for him to try to influence American opinion. In return Cheetham demanded an apology from the printer of the *Public Advertiser* and actually fought a duel with him, though Paine defiantly claimed responsibility for what he had said.

Thus far, Paine had the best of the exchange, but Cheetham soon found his opportunity in Paine's indiscretion. In the course of a conversation with William Coleman, editor of a Federalist paper, Paine had been foolish enough to quote a private letter from Jefferson, hinting at the possibility of a war with England. Coleman passed the word on, and Jefferson's remark appeared in print. Cheetham immediately accused Paine of having forged the letter.

Once more the Federalists whipped up a scandal, abusing the President for having confided in Paine. The friends of Jefferson were reduced to denying the letter, while Paine's retorted that it shed no discredit on the President. To Jefferson himself, the difficulties of a friendship with Paine must have been more evident than ever. No breach occurred between them, but the connection dwindled. All the leaders of the Republican Party respected his principles, but most of them had discontinued personal relations with him.

Early in 1807 Paine moved to another lodging, and in the following year he moved again several times. No difficulties arose between him and Jarvis, or elsewhere as far as is known; but he was restless and growing weaker in health. Probably he needed more comfort but did not want to pay enough to get it. Like many men who have been poor in childhood, he grew niggardly in old age. Actually his estate was still considerable; but he was living on his capital while trying in vain to raise old claims in Congress and worrying about the future of the Bonnevilles.

He seems to have suffered a series of small strokes or else a recurrence of the paralysis he had suffered in France. His appetite failed, and he grew weaker. Gradually he ceased to go out, but developed a pathetic eagerness to have people call. Even total strangers would do, as long as he had someone to talk to. The consequence is that we have a number of descriptions of him at this stage, of which the most vivid is that of an English visitor named Adams who found him sitting behind a table, "which was necessary to his support as he had received a paralytic stroke." He was trying to shave himself because the barber, though he lived not far away, refused to come in. There was nothing wrong with Paine's reasoning powers, and his dark eyes were keen and bright as ever. His conversation was sensible until it touched on politics or religion. On these subjects, about which he felt so deeply, he could no longer contain his emotion. His face flushed terribly, and the inflammation of his nose became disgusting.

He began to suffer from a swelling like dropsy which started at his feet and spread upward. He still did not think he required a doctor, but one came to see him and was joined by a colleague.

He made his will in January, 1809, his last piece of writing. In it he declared that he faced death with composure, conscious that he had spent his life in doing good. Soon afterward, he became bedridden. With some difficulty he persuaded Mme. Bonneville, who was regular in her visits, to take a house nearby in which to nurse him.

He was carried there in an armchair that May and died on the eighth of June, having three days before his death answered the question, "Do you *wish* to believe that Jesus Christ is the Son of God?" with a deliberate, "I have no wish to believe on that subject." Two clergymen who were convinced that he would not hold firm gained access to his bedroom on the last day of his life in the hopes of frightening him into renouncing his opinions. He still, however, had strength enough to say: "Let me alone. Good morning."

As his death approached, he had sent for a Quaker friend to ask permission to be buried in the Quaker cemetery. The church committee, however, refused, not out of hatred for his beliefs, but because they imagined his friends would wish to raise a memorial, which would be against their rules. Paine was deeply distressed, and Mme. Bonneville promised that he should be buried on his own farm.

"The farm will be sold," Paine objected, "and they will dig up my bones before they be half rotten."

Mme. Bonneville promised him that the plot at least should never be sold. On June 9, 1809, she and her son Benjamin and a few friends escorted the body to New Rochelle, where the interment took place. With a certain eloquence of feeling, she describes the event.

"Contemplating who it was, what man it was, that we were committing to an obscure grave on an open and disregarded bit of land, I could not help feeling most acutely. Before the earth was thrown down upon the coffin, I, placing myself at the east end of the grave, said to my son Benjamin, 'Stand you there at the other end as a witness for grateful America.' Looking round me, and beholding the small group of spectators, I exclaimed as the earth was tumbled into the grave, 'Oh! Mr. Paine! My son stands here as testimony of the gratitude of America, and I, for France.' "

What, then, of the gratitude of England? Ten years later William Cobbett, journalist, essayist, and radical of genius, visited the neglected spot and dug up the bones to convey them to England, where he thought to inter them in a suitable monument dedicated to the "common sense of the great man." Alas, he found no interest in his project. The bones were still with him when he died bankrupt and were passed from hand to hand until they were lost. Thus vanished forever Tom Paine, world citizen, claimed and rejected by three nations.

Epilogue

In the very year of Paine's death, his enemy Cheetham rushed into print with a biography whose scurrilous nature justified a good deal that Paine had said about him. He was not the first in the field. An Englishman named Chalmers, hired by Pitt's government to discredit the author of the *Rights,* had published a life of Paine in 1791. Both Cheetham and Chalmers took considerable pains to seem authentic and collected a number of unfavorable descriptions, connected by undoubted facts.

Paine's friends were slow to answer, perhaps because he had none who were really intimate with every stage of his life. Thomas Rickman, old acquaintance in Lewes and minor revolutionary poet, had known him again on his return to England. He wrote a biography in 1819, by which time many of his recollections were nearly fifty years old and his own powers were past their zenith. Another biographer who published in the same year had access to some American papers. French sources were not even consulted until the end of the century.

As a result, it has always been hard to do justice to Paine. Much of the personal material has been collected by men who wanted to do him harm. More rests on anecdotes from his own writings which sometimes look as though they had been embroidered on countless convivial evenings to make a good story. His was a character to which no one ever seemed indifferent. Men respected or despised him, admired or hated him with passion; but they were never merely fond or tolerant of him. Elizabeth Ollive, who might have helped us to know him better, guarded her relationship with her husband in dignified silence. Many who met him were less discreet. Their recollections were colored with the violence of their feelings.

These difficulties do not obscure the fact that Paine was an extraordinary person. Greatness, even genius he possessed; yet it was not the greatness which raises character above human weakness, nor was it the genius that involves capacity for taking pains. Perhaps the best measure of his quality may be found by comparing his failures in his own time with the success of his principles later.

Paine devoted his life to three great causes: the American Revolution, the Rights of Man, and the reform of religion. Of these, the American Revolution was successful, in part at least because it was not really the beginning of a golden age, but rather of a political structure reared, as Burke so truly saw, on the foundations of the past. The Rights of Man, which Paine attempted to embody in the French Revolution, failed utterly there. His reform of religion aroused resentment but did no serious damage to the churches.

In the light of these failures, it is interesting to see how much that Paine stood for in his own age is commonplace today. He was, for instance, the foe of privilege and heredity in politics, carrying his principles so far that he supported universal suffrage in a generation when even revolutionaries thought it impracticable. He perceived that the object of government should be the good of the governed, and he never excused it for oppressing the poor in the interest of maintaining order. Though his economics were unsound, he was convinced that government was capable of being treated as a rational science and that it need not be a hodge-podge of compromises worked out by trial and error. In these and similar ways the influence of what he wrote and thought did not die with him. It would be going too far to say that Paine created the age of the common man, but he certainly provided its basic inspiration. He gave it coherent thoughts which the circumstances of later generations were to develop. Thus despite his outmoded historical judgments, Paine is a more modern man than his contemporaries.

On religion he had less effect. Indeed, to all practical purposes it is hard to say that he had any. Yet he was a pioneer among those who were to examine doctrine by the light of reason rather than revelation. Science is accepted in our day as a reliable method of checking what we believe. Those who study the effect of science on religion speak of Darwin rather than Paine. They discuss the particular impact of the theory of evolution on traditional belief. They are right to do so. Yet if we measure Paine by the clarity of his thinking rather than by its historical effect, he has at least the distinction of foreseeing that reason will have a role in the religious beliefs of the future.

Such were the successes which justify Paine's fame, yet they did not cause it. All his other gifts would have been nothing without his ability to reduce an argument to essentials and to present these in language which was instantly memorable. Paine's punctuation is slipshod, his grammar is sometimes careless; but he is a master of English prose, remarkably readable not merely in his own day, but almost two centuries later. What is more, he can even now play upon the emotions. His vision of the ideal state is still appealing. His compassion for the downtrodden is still warm.

What Paine conveys to us is the fact that his convictions were deeply genuine. Intellectuals like John Adams despised the way he got them, picking them up here or there in conversation without troubling to track down their origins. Truth was, Paine had an attitude to life; and he fitted into it such ideas as came his way. In this fashion he preserved unity of thought far better than those who make a study of fragments of knowledge and then try to match them with one another. Intellectually he was a whole man, and his satisfactions were found almost entirely in that sphere. His human weaknesses contrasted with the inner security which he found only in fundamentals.

He never was able to understand the position of anyone else because to do so he would have had to pretend he was not himself. Something basic in him made this impossible; and it accounted for a tranquil self-satisfaction which too often under the stresses of practical life became mere vanity. In some respects he was an unhappy man, lonely and beset by failings which caused more trouble to himself than to anyone else. It stood to reason that he would die in obscurity and be buried unnoticed. Yet he always felt that his life was justified, and history on the whole agrees with his verdict.

Suggestions for Wider Reading

Foner, Philip S. (ed.). *The Complete Writings of Thomas Paine*. New York, Citadel, 1945. This contains the major works of Paine mentioned in this book.

Aldridge, Alfred Owen. *Man of Reason*. Philadelphia, Lippincott, 1959. By far the most scholarly life of Paine.

Conway, Moncure D. *The Life of Thomas Paine*. New York, Putnam, 1892. This earliest good biography of Paine is long out of print, but is in some libraries.

Fast, Howard. *Citizen Tom Paine*. New York, Duell, 1943. This vivid and exciting novel does not stick to the known facts of Paine's life and character. (Also published in paperback by Bantam.)

Burke, Edmund. *Reflections on the Revolution in France*. Originally published in London in 1791, there are many editions, some in paperback.

GENERAL BACKGROUND

United States, 1774-1809. There are far too many books on this period to list, but some that may be easily available are:

Morison, Samuel Eliot. *The Oxford History of the American People*. New York, Oxford, 1965.

Faÿ, Bernard. *Franklin, the Apostle of Modern Times*. Boston, Little, 1929.

Van Doren, Carl. *Benjamin Franklin*. New York, Viking, 1938.

Padover, Saul K. *Thomas Jefferson and the Foundations of American Freedom.* Princeton, Van Nostrand. (An Anvil paperback.)

Little, Shelby. *George Washington.* New York, Minton, Balch, 1929. (Also published by Putnam as a Capricorn paperback.)

France, 1789-1802. Also covered briefly in the works on England listed below.

Eimerl, Sarel. *Revolution: France 1789-1794.* Boston, Little, 1967. A book for young readers which gives a clear outline of events.

Loomis, Stanley. *Paris in the Terror.* Philadelphia, Lippincott, 1964. Vivid descriptions of Marat, Danton, and Robespierre.

Thompson, J. M. *The French Revolution.* New York, Oxford, 1945. (Also published by Oxford as a Galaxy paperback.)

England, 1737-1809, and general history.

Churchill, Winston S. *A History of the English-Speaking Peoples.* Vol. 3, *The Age of Revolution.* New York, Dodd, 1957.

Trevelyan, G. M. *History of England.* London, Longmans, 1926. (Also published by Doubleday as an Anchor paperback.)

Ward, A. W. (ed.). *The Cambridge Modern History,* Vols. 7 and 8. New York, Macmillan, 1907. A detailed and scholarly reference book.

Index

JB P		24733
Coolidge, Olivia		
AUTHOR		
Tom Paine, Revolutionary		
TITLE		

DATE LOANED	BORROWER'S NAME	DATE RETURNED
MAY 17 '73	B Z Steinrage	JUN 11 '73
APR 26 '74	Diane Horowitz	MAY 29 '74
OCT 20 '75	M. Adams	OCT 29 '75